Cybersecurity in Robotic Autonomous Vehicles

Cybersecurity in Robotic Autonomous Vehicles introduces a novel intrusion detection system (IDS) specifically designed for AVs, which leverages data prioritisation in CAN IDs to enhance threat detection and mitigation. It offers a pioneering intrusion detection model for AVs that uses machine and deep learning algorithms.

Presenting a new method for improving vehicle security, the book demonstrates how the IDS has incorporated machine learning and deep learning frameworks to analyse CAN bus traffic and identify the presence of any malicious activities in real time with high level of accuracy. It provides a comprehensive examination of the cybersecurity risks faced by AVs with a particular emphasis on CAN vulnerabilities and the innovative use of data prioritisation within CAN IDs.

The book will interest researchers and advanced undergraduate students taking courses in cybersecurity, automotive engineering, and data science. Automotive industry and robotics professionals focusing on Internet of Vehicles and cybersecurity will also benefit from the contents.

Cybersecurity in Robotic Autonomous Vehicles

Machine Learning Applications to Detect Cyber Attacks

Ahmed Alruwaili, Sardar M.N. Islam
and Iqbal Gondal

CRC Press
Taylor & Francis Group
Boca Raton London New York

CRC Press is an imprint of the
Taylor & Francis Group, an **informa** business

First edition published 2025
by CRC Press
2385 NW Executive Center Drive, Suite 320, Boca Raton FL 33431

and by CRC Press
4 Park Square, Milton Park, Abingdon, Oxon, OX14 4RN

CRC Press is an imprint of Taylor & Francis Group, LLC

ISBN: 978-1-041-00640-4 (hbk)
ISBN: 978-1-003-61091-5 (pbk)
ISBN: 978-1-003-61090-8 (ebk)

DOI: 10.1201/9781003610908

Typeset in Times
by Apex CoVantage, LLC

Contents

Preface

Technology has developed at a very fast rate in the recent past, and this has greatly impacted society in aspects such as communication and transport. One of the most innovative technologies is the Internet of Vehicles (IoV), which can change the world of transportation and build a system of autonomous and intelligent vehicles connected to an interconnected network. However, with the increased connectivity arises a new cybersecurity challenge that stems from the fact that vehicles are now susceptible to cyber threats that can threaten their safety, reliability, and efficiency. These challenges form the core motivation for this book: the urgent need to develop robust cybersecurity solutions for autonomous vehicles (AVs) operating within the IoV ecosystem.

Some of the most critical bus systems used in modern vehicles are the controller area network (CAN). CAN bus is the network which controls the flow of information between the electronic control units (ECUs) within the vehicle. Although it is a crucial component in managing the overall functioning of AVs, the CAN bus was not developed with security as a consideration. Its lack of security mechanisms exposes vehicles to serious vulnerabilities, including message injection attacks. In such attacks, hackers can inject malicious commands into the CAN bus, which leads the ECUs to perform certain actions that they were not supposed to, which may lead to malfunctions, accidents, or even fatalities. CAN bus is its reliance on message prioritisation based on CAN IDs. Lower CAN ID values are prioritised for transmission, which presents an opportunity for attackers to manipulate high-priority messages and disrupt the normal functioning of the vehicle. This calls for new strategies to address this threat that cannot be solved by conventional security measures.

In response to these challenges, this book introduces a novel intrusion detection system (IDS) specifically designed for AVs, which leverages data prioritisation in CAN IDs to enhance threat detection and mitigation. To be more precise, the IDS analyses the sequence of CAN bus messages and filters the data flow, which increases the efficiency of anomaly and cyber threat detection. We have incorporated machine learning and deep learning frameworks into the IDS in order to analyse CAN bus traffic and identify the presence of any malicious activities in real time with a high level of accuracy. By employing classifiers like support vector machines (SVM), k-nearest neighbours (KNN), and neural networks, the system has been able to maintain an accuracy rate of more than 99% in identifying between the genuine data and the possible threats with minimal false alarms.

This book provides a comprehensive examination of the cybersecurity risks faced by AVs, with a particular emphasis on CAN vulnerabilities and the innovative use of data prioritisation within CAN IDs. Through filling the research gap between the theoretical studies and practical implementations, it offers a new method for improving vehicle security. This approach is not only beneficial for researchers but also offers industry professionals helpful methods that can be used to protect actual AV systems. Readers will find this book invaluable as both a reference guide and a practical manual for improving the cybersecurity of autonomous vehicles. Researchers can use the models and frameworks presented here to further advance the field of vehicular cybersecurity, exploring new directions in data prioritisation and attack detection. These solutions can be used by industry professionals and engineers to improve the safety of current and future autonomous vehicle networks, making the IDS system flexible for use in various aspects of the IoV.

About the Authors

Mr. Ahmed Alruwaili is a researcher specialising in cyber security, artificial intelligence, and quantum computing. He received his Bachelor of Computer Science in computer science and information from Aljouf University, Saudi Arabia, in 2013, and a Master of Information Technology with a focus on cyber security from Deakin University, Australia, in 2019. Currently, he is pursuing his PhD at Victoria University, Australia, where he focuses on enhancing security frameworks for the Internet of Vehicles. His research bridges theoretical concepts and practical applications in areas such as cyber security, artificial intelligence, game theory, distributed systems security, machine autonomy, and quantum computing. An active member of the Institute for Systems and Technologies of Information, Control and Communication (INSTICC), and the Australian Information Security Association (AISA), Mr. Alruwaili is committed to contributing to the academic community and staying at the forefront of developments in his field.

Dr. Sardar M. N. Islam (Naz) is currently a professor at Victoria University, Australia. He is also a distinguished visiting professor of artificial intelligence at UnSri and a distinguished visiting professor of quantum technologies and computing at BIT; adjunct professor of IT and business at Armstrong Institute, Melbourne; and editor-in-chief of *International Transactions on Artificial Intelligence*. Professor Islam adopts a global and humanistic approach in his research and academic works. He has published 31 scholarly authored academic books and 4 edited books with prestigious international publishers in different disciplines, including computer science. Professor Islam has also published approx. 250 articles, including some of the leading international journal articles in his specialised research areas.

Dr. Iqbal Gondal is Associate Dean in Cloud, Systems and Security, and Deputy Director (cybersecurity) Sir Lawrence Wackett Defence & Aerospace Centre (SLWDAC) in Royal Melbourne Institute of Technology (RMIT), Australia. He has worked in industry and academia for 25 years in both Singapore and Australia. He was the director of Internet Commerce Security Lab (ICSL) for seven years to conduct translational research in cybersecurity. Previously, he was the director of ICT strategy for the faculty of IT in Monash, India. He is a fellow of Institute of Engineers Australia, member of IEEE USA, and graduate member of Australian Institute of Company Directors (GAICD). Dr. Gondal worked as a research fellow and a senior software systems engineer for seven years in Singapore and Australia with Delphi (GM), Singapore Manufacturing Technology (SimTech) centre, and other industries working on design and development, project management, system design and integration, SCADA, intelligent techniques, adaptive systems, and wireless switches for financial services. He has published over 219-refereed conference and journal papers, and he is a an experienced HDR supervisor. Dr. Gondal was a member of the University Governing Council & Engineering Advisory Committee, Non-Exec Director of Oceania Cyber Security Centre, and University engagement for the Defence Science Institute.

Figures

Tables

Abbreviations

ACK	Acknowledge
AVs	Autonomous vehicles
CAN	Controller area network
CNN	Convolutional neural network
CRC	Cyclic redundancy check
DBN	Deep belief network
DCNN	Deep convolutional neural network
DDoS	Distributed denial of service
DEL	Delimiter
DL	Deep learning
DLC	Data length code
DNN	Deep neural network
DT	Decision tree
ECUs	Electrical control units
EDP	Extended data page
ELM	Extreme learning machine
EOF	End of frame
FN	False negative
FP	False positive
GAN	Generative adversarial network
GPS	Global positioning system
GRU	Gated recurrent units
ID	Identifier
IDE	Identifier extension
IDS	Intrusion detection system
IFS	Inter frame space
IID	Identically distributed
IoT	Internet of Things
IoV	Internet of Vehicles
IVN	Intra-vehicle networks
KNN	K-nearest neighbour
LIN	Local interconnect network
LSTM	Long short-term memory
MARL	Multi-agent reinforcement learning

MAS	Multi-agent system
ML	Machine learning
MOST	Media Oriented Systems Transport
NHTSA	National Highway Traffic Safety Administration
NN	Neural network
Rbf	Radial basis function
RF	Random forest
RNN	Recurrent neural network
RPM	Radiation portal monitors
RTR	Remote transmission request
SOF	Start of frame
SVM	Support vector machine
TML	Traditional machine learning
TN	True negative
TP	True positive
VANETs	Vehicular ad hoc networks
V2C	Vehicle-to-Cloud
V2I	Vehicle-to-Infrastructure
V2T	Vehicle-to-Personal Device
V2R	Vehicle-to-Roadside
V2S	Vehicle-to-Sensors
V2V	Vehicle-to-Vehicle

Introduction 1

1.1 BACKGROUND

In the modern era concerning the development of distributed autonomous systems, machines have become more independent and productive in their operations, which has led to the emergence of a new concept known as "multi-agent systems". Ferber and Gutknecht [1] define multi-agent systems as a group of agents interacting together in the same environment to achieve a goal. The agent has the ability to make a decision based on its interaction with the surrounding environment, thus achieving independence and enhancing intelligence [2]. The features of these systems are characterised by agency, independence, negotiation, cooperation, communication, and interaction [2]. These systems are used widely in many fields, such as computer science and engineering [3]. These systems are linked according to the field of their use.

In the past few years, new integrated technologies have changed many different fields and turned them into more advanced data communication systems called the Internet of Things (IoT). These technologies include smart homes, smart health, and smart transportation systems [4]. According to recent estimates, the number of devices connected to the Internet has increased to 25 billion [5]. With the increase in the number of vehicles connected to the Internet, IoT presented a new theme in the vehicular networks field, known as the Internet of Vehicles (IoV) [6]. The IoV is a networked, open, and integrated system with controllability, operationalisation, credibility, and high manageability. It is an integration of multiple agents such as vehicles, users, things, and networks [7]. This integration between the intelligent multi-agents for the IoV has some advantages and disadvantages during communication and interaction between the parties.

One of the key areas where the IoV network is expected to have a significant impact is in the field of robotics. As a technology field, robotics deals with the design, construction, operation, and application of robots. Robots are

DOI: 10.1201/9781003610908-1

machines that can perform a series of complex actions automatically, often programmed by a computer [8]. According to [9], robots have several key properties that distinguish them from other machines, including their ability to sense their environment, move and manipulate objects, and make decisions based on their programming and sensor data. The advantages of robotics are many, and these include their ability to work consistently and accurately, operate in hazardous or inaccessible environments, and perform tasks that are too dangerous or tedious for humans [10].

The usage of robots has increased significantly in recent years, and they are being used in different sectors such as manufacturing, health care, agriculture, and transportation. In the transportation industry, robotics is being used to facilitate individual mobility, particularly through autonomous vehicles [11]. Autonomous vehicles can drive and navigate without human intervention, so they are made possible through the integration of various technologies, such as multi-agent systems (MAS), the IoT, and vehicular networks (VANET), which make up the Internet of Vehicles network [7]. Different types of robots are being used in various industries, such as industrial robots in manufacturing, service robots in cleaning and security, and medical robots in surgical and other medical procedures. The potential of robotics is vast, and it offers numerous opportunities for innovation. Therefore, this research highlights the emergence of the IoV network and its impact on the field of robotics, specifically on autonomous vehicles.

Since the number of vehicles connected to the Internet is growing, the amount of data from the vehicles' networks are increasing as well [12]. Many modern vehicles have a certain level of automation, such as a lane-keeping framework, adaptive cruise control, crash-warning systems, self-parking technology, etc. [13]. In the next few years, fully autonomous vehicles will be available for individuals [14]. These refinements will encourage individuals to adopt autonomous vehicles to facilitate mobility, especially for those who do not drive because of age or disability.

Network communications are frequently employed in intra-vehicle networks (IVN) [15]. IVN systems need to connect to the Internet more frequently as a result of the IoV technology's rapid growth; in order to provide online communication and real-time traffic updates. In addition, autonomous vehicles (AVs) contain multiple electrical control units (ECUs) communicating through different protocols and busses. These buses include controller area network (CAN), FlexRay, local interconnect network (LIN), or the Media Oriented Systems Transport (MOST) [16]. Figure 1.1 illustrates the typical IVN architecture. The FlexRay and MOST have proven that they are faster than CAN but are more expensive. Consequently, our research will focus on CAN in the internal context of autonomous vehicles.

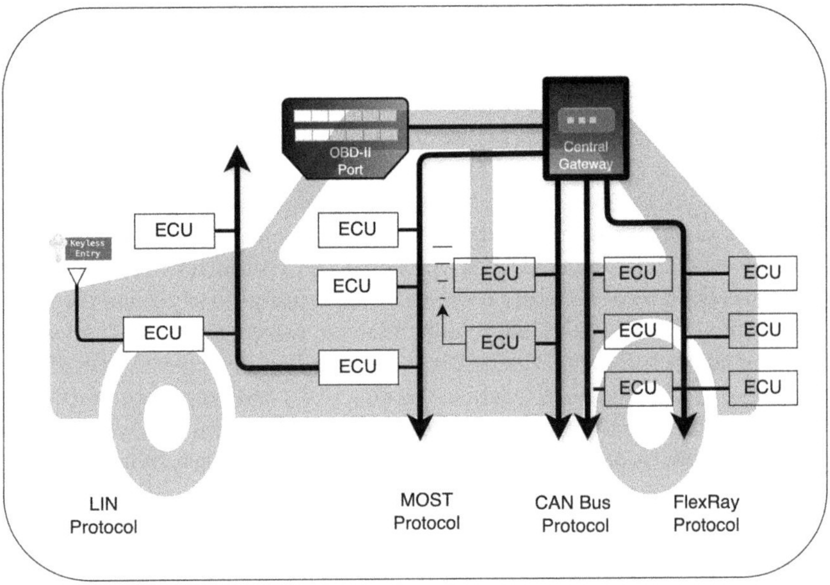

FIGURE 1.1 The typical in-vehicle network architecture

1.2 SCOPE

Autonomous vehicles contain a variety of communication technologies that can be used for entertainment, customer service, diagnostics, and internal control. Any of these technologies might be used as a threat by the malicious users. This book focuses on internal communication security, specifically in the CAN bus.

1.3 PROBLEM

Despite the enormous benefits of autonomous vehicles, many studies have shown that AVs can have a negative impact on drivers' security, privacy, and quality of life [7, 17]. This is because the AV systems, including the CAN bus, transmit data between ECUs. These ECUs manage vehicle subsystems such as gearbox, engine, speed, airbag, etc. The transmitted data between ECUs through CAN bus faces security challenges like data encryption and user authentication, which will affect the CAN bus security system [18]. This means the data will be vulnerable because it is coming from different nodes. One of these nodes could be used to perform a distributed denial of service (DDoS) attack to take the network down. Hackers could take control of AVs, resulting in traffic collisions and devastating consequences, including death [17, 19]. Thus, the lack of security protections like user authentication and message encryption makes the ECUs in the CAN bus vulnerable to cyber-attacks. These factors emphasise the critical necessity for security mechanisms to safeguard the CAN bus essential [6]. Recently, one solution that has gained researchers' attention for reducing such security challenges is the intrusion detection system (IDS), which is a process that uses machine learning (ML) and deep learning (DL) to monitor the CAN bus network [14]. This involves monitoring data sent between the different ECUs and alerting the system to any suspicious activity.

1.4 SIGNIFICANCE AND PRACTICAL IMPORTANCE OF THIS RESEARCH

This research can demonstrate its significance in many situations. By protecting IoV from cyber threats, it may deter the possibility of severe damage to people and infrastructure and prevent governments from losing a lot of money. This research will contribute to the subject by improving the training model by reducing the time required for training and enhancing the quality of data. This will enhance the safety of the vehicle network and the system for moving people in the real world. As far as we know, there is no work published yet that classifies transmitted messages on CAN bus for effective intrusion detection system.

1.5 RESEARCH AIMS AND RESEARCH QUESTIONS

This research aims to devise an intrusion detection system that uses ML and DL to recognise whether the data originates from a real node or a hacker node connected to the CAN bus. This research addresses the following research question: "How can machine learning and deep learning be leveraged to enhance the cybersecurity of autonomous vehicles communication, considering the dynamic and complex nature of AVs networks and the threat landscape?"

Objectives:

- To investigate the current state of cybersecurity in AV networks and identify the major threats and vulnerabilities that pose a risk to their communication.
- To explore the potential of machine learning and deep learning techniques in enhancing the cybersecurity of AV networks and mitigating the identified threats.
- To develop a machine learning and deep learning-based IDS for detecting cybersecurity threats in AV networks.
- To evaluate the performance and effectiveness of the proposed solution through a series of experiments.
- To identify the limitations and challenges associated with using machine learning and deep learning in AV cybersecurity and propose recommendations for future research.

The research will provide valuable insights into the design and optimisation of IDSs for AVs and help enhance the overall cybersecurity of AV networks. The proposed IDS prototype can be integrated into existing AV systems to provide effective protection against cyber-attacks.

1.6 METHODOLOGY OF THE RESEARCH

The research methodology is divided into two parts. The first part conducts an extensive literature review search on the evolution of autonomous vehicle security and understanding of in-vehicle network architecture and CAN security methods through in-vehicle IDS design. In the second part, we will first choose a public dataset that includes the CAN messages that have been attacked on the network. Second, the dataset will be analysed and processed to implement the IDS. This is followed by devising a lightweight IDS capable of detecting security threats in the CAN bus network. The need for a lightweight IDS is crucial for the security of AVs since they rely on low-power units with limited computational capabilities. Finally, the effectiveness of IDS in detecting attacks will be evaluated by measuring the incidence of true positive, false positive, true negative, and false negative results.

1.7 CONTRIBUTIONS OF THE BOOK

The following are the main contributions of this book:

- In this book, a novel model which is based on the nature of the AV data has been proposed. The proposed model distinguishes all high-priority messages for training the deep learning algorithms. At the same time, all low-priority messages are used for machine learning algorithms.
- The proposed architecture ensures the continuous flow of high and low-priority data, with no collisions.
- Proposed techniques classification performance in detecting threats on the CAN bus network has been compared with well know models.
- Our work contributes to the field of intrusion detection by addressing two critical challenges: minimising classification errors and reducing the computational burden of the system. By employing a balanced class and a limited number of attributes, we aim to improve the accuracy of intrusion detection while ensuring that the system can operate efficiently on low-power devices commonly used in autonomous vehicles.

1.8 BOOK OUTLINE

This book is organised into six chapters. Chapter 1 is a description of the study's background, scope, problem, research aim, research questions, and methodology. Chapter 2 presents an overview of the literature on multi-agent systems, Internet of Vehicles, and autonomous vehicles specification as the theoretical basis of our research. In-depth information about the CAN bus protocol and intrusion detection system presented in Chapter 3, which describes the method used to mitigate the vulnerabilities in the CAN bus protocol. Chapter 4 explains the proposed solution and presents details of the implementation steps. Chapter 5 covers the relevant results and discussion regarding the research question. Finally, the conclusion of the book and future research ideas on this topic are stated in Chapter 6.

Theoretical Lens 2

2.1 MULTI-AGENT SYSTEMS

Multi-agent systems (MAS) are defined as agents interacting in the same environment to achieve a certain goal [1]. MAS is an application, and it operates independently in an environment using protocols and languages to interact with other agents [20]. The individual agent has the ability to make a decision based on his interaction with the surrounding environment and so in this way achieves independence and intelligence [2]. Furthermore, it has some features that are characterised by agency, independence, negotiation, cooperation, communication, and interaction [2]. These systems are used widely in many fields [3] and are linked according to the field of their use. This section focuses on the communication, application, and learning aspects of MAS.

Communication in multi-agent systems is an important component. Failure of the connection can mean consequences and increases the cost to the agent [21]. MAS features are a particular mechanism that makes them simple to implement and that can handle complicated protocols for interaction with the vehicle to communicate with the environment [22]. These systems were examined by Campos-Rodriguez et al. [2], who identified aspects that might impact the distributed network system, and they considered vehicles and infrastructure (such as corridors, signals, pedestrians, etc.) as agents. Communications can be classified into multiple systems. Agents are referred to as local communication [23, 24], blackboard [25], or mobile communications, which fall under local communications. However, MAS can be used to develop distributed applications for complex systems [2].

Regarding MAS applications, Campos-Rodriguez et al. [2] reviewed the applications of multi-agent systems in the automotive industry, focusing on traffic regulation and road balancing. Müller and Fischer [26] investigated 152 applications across industries that made use of MAS methods. Both Kober et al.

DOI: 10.1201/9781003610908-2

[27], who looked at robotic control, and Shakshuki and Reid [28], who explored multi-agent applications in the healthcare business, have shown that there are efficient reinforcement learning (RL) methodologies that can be applied to robots in the real world. However, Derakhshan and Yousefi [29] in their research concentrated on the applications that use wireless sensor networks.

The relationship between multi-agent systems and artificial intelligence has attracted the interest of many researchers. Artificial intelligence has led to the development of new methods (e.g., machine learning) that make it easier for researchers to devise complex data analytics applications. Agent learning is defined as the process of training an agent by entering information, results, and procedures to ensure that he achieves a specific goal. This process is carried out through three methods: active learning, interactive learning, and consequence-based learning [30]. Machine learning algorithms have accurate characteristics and also have advantages and drawbacks in producing models that perform classification, regression, clustering, and behavioural learning. Hernandez-Leal et al. [31] presented a new classification for deep multi-agent emerging RL techniques based on a summary of how classical MAS research concepts, including behaviour, learning communication, and opponent modelling were merged into deep multi-agent reinforcement learning (MARL) domains. Challenges in multi-agent learning such as partial observability, continuous state and action spaces, and transfer learning were examined by Nguyen et al. [32]. The use of deep MARL approaches in fully cooperative games was examined in depth by Oroojlooy and Hajinezhad [33]. Zhang et al. [34] conducted a targeted literature review to find MARL algorithms with theoretical convergence guarantees and complexity analysis.

Multi-agent systems have shown their suitability as a solution for distributed systems such as automated vehicles. However, MAS does have certain challenges such as the interaction between agents, which remains a serious issue because it passes messages (containing personal information) between the agents [2], and as a result, it breaks the information's confidentiality. Nevertheless, our study will not attempt to fix these issues since they are outside its scope. MAS was mentioned to understand the concept behind the Internet of Vehicles, which will be explained next.

2.2 AN OVERVIEW OF INTERNET OF VEHICLES

In recent years, new integrated technologies have transformed many diverse industries into advanced data communication networks referred to as the Internet of Things (IoT), which is applied in different fields such as smart houses, smart transportation systems, and smart health systems [4]. This integration has increased the number of devices connected to the Internet to 25 billion [8], including vehicles. As a result, the concept of the Internet of Vehicles (IoV) is now part of vehicular networks [6]. IoV is an open, integrated network system with controllability, operability, reliability, and high manageability, which integrates several agents such as vehicles, users, objects, and networks [7]. However, this integration between the intelligent multi-agents may give the IoV some advantages and disadvantages regarding communication and interaction between the parties. This section will discover the progress made in communication that led to the IoV and subsequent security challenges.

Several studies had focused on the classifications of communication in IoV. Abu Talib, Abbas [35] categorised the IoV's communication into three types: Vehicle-to-Infrastructure (V2I), communication between vehicles and road infrastructure, such as traffic signals and road sensors; Vehicle-to-Vehicle (V2V), direct communication between vehicles to share information about traffic conditions, hazards, and other relevant data; and Vehicle-to-Cloud (V2C), communication between vehicles and cloud services for data storage, processing, and access to various applications. While Sharma presented the most comprehensive classification of IoV's communication, Chauhan [36] categorised IoV's communication into five categories: Vehicle-to-Vehicle (V2V); Vehicle-to-Sensors (V2S), communication with sensors within or around the vehicle; Vehicle-to-Infrastructure (V2I); Vehicle-to-Roadside Units (V2R), interaction with roadside units that facilitate data exchange; and Vehicle-to-Personal Devices (V2T), communication with personal devices such as smartphones and wearables [36]. On the other hand, a study by Yang and Wang [7] proposed the IoV network model. Figure 2.1 illustrates the IoV network model proposed, divided into two parts: an individual model and a swarm model. The individual model is the interactions that occur in one vehicle, whether the interactions between a human with an environment, a vehicle with an environment or things with an environment. This model focuses on the interactions within the vehicle's intra-network. The swarm model focuses on scenarios with multiple humans, vehicles, objects, and networks, where IoV provides services and applications through swarm intelligence, crowd sourcing, and crowd sensing [7].

A human is referred to as any person connected to the IoV, whether drivers, passengers, or beneficiaries of road services, such as pedestrians or cyclists. Vehicles are referred to as all connected vehicles that benefit from the services provided by the IoV, and they are vehicles with computing and storage capabilities that can connect to the Internet. The term "things" refers to any device connected to the IoV other than humans and vehicles, including light signals, sensors, etc. Environment refers to an environment where interactions between the user, vehicles, and objects take place. Many challenges potentially arise as a result of these interactions in IoV communications.

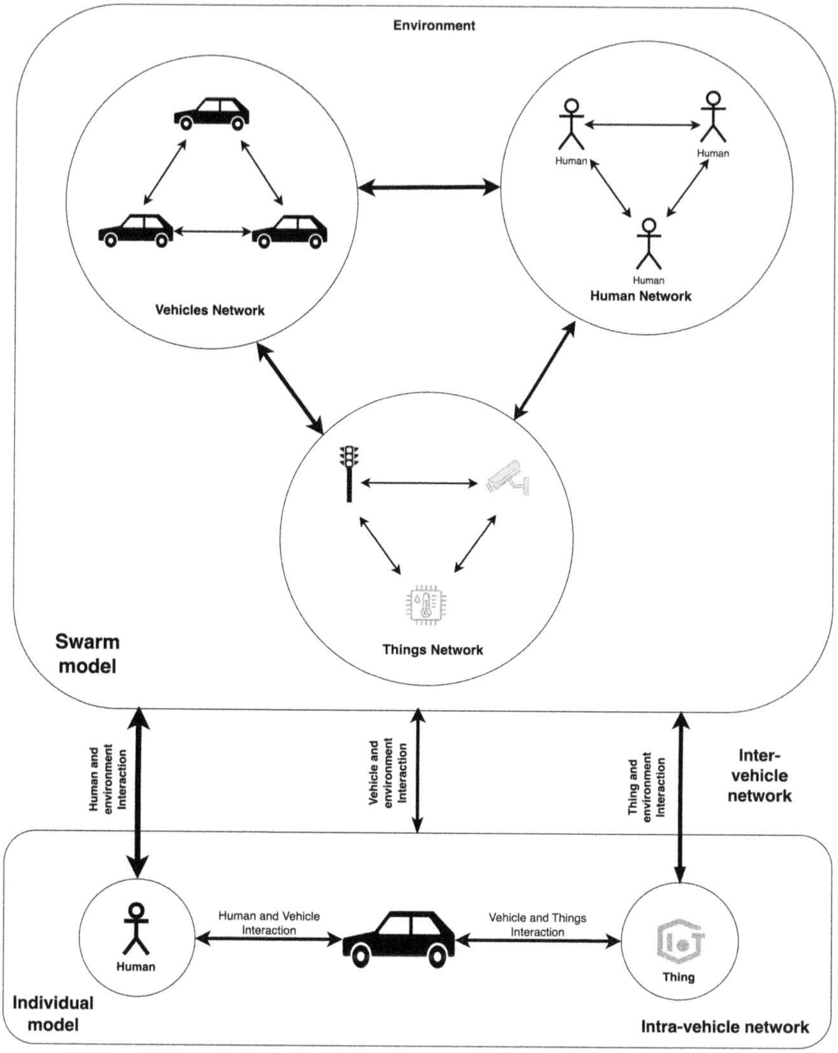

FIGURE 2.1 The IoV network model

The integration of many technologies, standards, and services into the vehicular Internet has led to security challenges such as the complexity in carrying out its tasks, as it must connect users, other vehicles, and infrastructure consisting of numerous networks [22]. According to Zhang and Wu [37], IoV contains many vulnerabilities due to its insecure environment. The exploitation of data flows by malicious people through vulnerabilities can have devastating effects [38]. Hickey [39] reviewed the mitigation techniques used in infrastructure systems because of their feasibility in analysing the security problem from the perspective of effort and impact. Zhang and Wu [37] proposed a location-based service programme to solve security and privacy challenges. Similarly, Rivas and Barceló-Ordinas [38] attempted to solve the security problems of vehicular ad hoc networks (VANETs) by surveying the latest trends and concluded the security challenges that should be considered are security, misbehaving and faulty nodes, and secure data aggregation. On the other hand, Sun and Wu [17] discussed the security and privacy in IoV. They classified the attack in IoV into five types: attacks on authentication, availability attacks, secrecy attacks, routing attacks, and data authenticity attacks.

Most studies have shown the importance of detecting possible threats to IoV communication [13]. The study published in 2019 investigated cyber security threats to wireless vehicle networks, responses, and challenges [40]. Abu Talib et al. [35] explored the security threats, responses, and potential challenges in the VANETs and IoV domains. Zhou et al. [41] claim that machine learning algorithms on IoV can improve their efficiency by utilising the federal learning model. In conclusion, each of these threats has corresponding implementation methods and security requirements to ensure security in IoV. However, our research endeavours will focus on autonomous vehicle security since it is an important issue.

2.3 ROBOTICS

Robotics is the branch of technology that deals with robot design, construction, operation, and application [8]. A robot serves as an apparatus intended to perform intricate functions independently from human control. Robots have several key properties that distinguish them from other machines. These properties include the ability to sense their environment, to move and manipulate objects, and make decisions based on their programming and the data they collect from their sensors. Some of the key advantages of robotics include their ability to work accurately and consistently, operate in hazardous or inaccessible environments, and perform tasks that are too dangerous or tedious for humans. There are several different types of robots, including industrial robots, which are used in manufacturing and other industrial settings; service robots, which are used for tasks such as cleaning and security; and medical robots, which are used for surgical and other medical procedures. Robotics can be used in a variety of fields, including manufacturing, health care, agriculture, and transportation [10]. In the transportation industry, robotics is being used to facilitate the individual's mobility as autonomous vehicles, which are vehicles that are capable of navigating and driving without human intervention.

2.4 AUTONOMOUS VEHICLES

As the prevalence of Internet-connected automobiles increases, so does the volume of data within their networks [12]. Numerous contemporary vehicles possess varying degrees of automation, such as lane maintenance systems, adaptive speed regulators, collision alerts, and self-parking capabilities [13]. The National Highway Traffic Safety Administration (NHTSA) has classified these automation stages into six distinct levels, from zero automation to entirely automated vehicles, as illustrated in Figure 2.2 [42].

In the forthcoming future, fully autonomous vehicles will be accessible for personal use [14]. These advancements will likely incentivise individuals to embrace self-driving cars, enhancing mobility for those who are unable to drive due to age or disability. The development of autonomous vehicles is occurring rapidly and significantly influencing both society and individuals. However, certain obstacles may hinder their widespread adoption. Despite the numerous advantages of self-driving vehicles, they may adversely affect driver safety, privacy, and overall well-being.

Autonomous vehicles are engineered to operate and navigate independently, without the need for human direction. They utilise sensor data and artificial intelligence to adapt to their surrounding environment. As vehicles' autonomy level escalates, the quantity of electronic control units (ECUs), also known as sensors, augments. These ECUs disseminate data via numerous protocols, with the controller area network (CAN bus) being the most renowned. Despite the vast potential of the CAN bus, elevated sophistication may give rise to amplified security risks. Given that data is derived from multiple nodes, one of these nodes could potentially be exploited by a hacker intending to

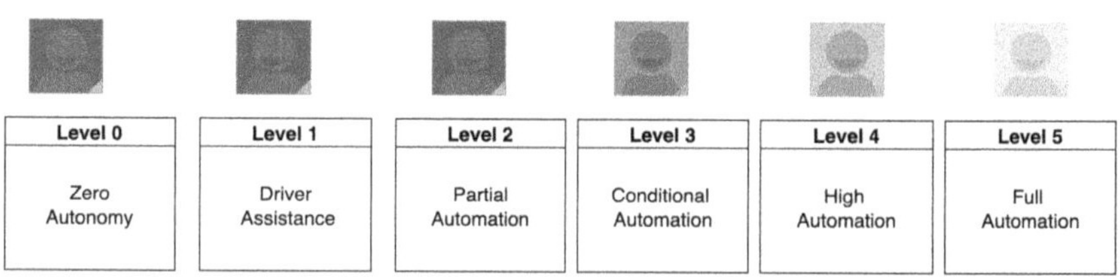

FIGURE 2.2 The automation levels introduced by NHTSA

TABLE 2.1 The similarities between robotics and autonomous vehicles

	ROBOTIC	*AUTONOMOUS VEHICLES*
The development of advanced technologies for automating complex tasks	This involves designing and constructing robots capable of performing a wide range of functions, such as manufacturing, cleaning, surgery, and more.	This involves the development of vehicles that are capable of navigating and driving without human input.
Rely on sensors and other technologies for perception and decision-making	Sensors allow robots to gather information about their environment and make decisions about how to move and interact with objects.	Sensors such as cameras, LiDAR, and radar are used to gather information about the vehicle's surroundings and make decisions about navigating and avoiding obstacles.
Rely on advanced algorithms and machine learning techniques to process the data sensors collect and make decisions	Machine learning algorithms enable robots to learn from experience and improve their performance over time.	Machine learning algorithms enable the vehicle to learn from its experiences on the road and improve its decision-making capabilities.
The potential to revolutionise the way we live and work	This includes the potential to automate many tasks that are currently performed by humans, which could lead to increased productivity and efficiency in a variety of industries.	This includes the potential to improve the safety and efficiency of the transportation system, which could lead to reduced traffic congestion and fewer accidents on the road.

initiate a distributed denial of service (DDoS) attack, thereby destabilising the network. Cybercriminals could seize control of intelligent vehicles, leading to disastrous traffic accidents and potentially causing fatalities [17, 19].

The relationship between robotics and autonomous vehicles is close, as many of the technologies used in autonomous vehicles, such as sensors, machine learning algorithms, and advanced control systems, are also used in robotics. In fact, many of the key components of autonomous vehicles, such as the cameras, light detection and ranging (LiDAR) sensors, and radar sensors that are used for perception and localisation, are based on technologies that were originally developed for use in robotics [10]. Table 2.1 shows the similarities between robotic and autonomous vehicles.

Overall, robotics and autonomous vehicle technologies are similar as both rely on similar technologies like sensors and machine learning algorithms, and both have potential to revolutionise how we live and work. Both fields are rapidly evolving and are likely to continue to have a major impact on a wide range of industries in the coming years.

Exploring CAN Bus Security 3

Insights and Analysis

3.1 CONTROLLER AREA NETWORK

Data within the car's internal network is transmitted and sent through four protocols, the most famous being the control area network (CAN), which is cost-effective, resistant to electrical interference, and has the ability to correct errors. The advantage of the CAN bus lies in the transmission speed at a connection rate of 1Mbps [43]. Accordingly, it is widely used in modern automobile factories. CAN was developed in 1986 by Robert Bosch. CAN has been used in a wide range of systems, such as medical instruments, industrial control systems, and modern vehicles, since the publication of the ISO 11898 standard in 1994 [15].

In modern autonomous vehicles, nodes are electronic control units (ECUs), which communicate through CAN bus broadcasts. CAN bus message frames are 111 bits long, with the first bit being the start of frame (SOF), followed by an arbitration field of 12 bits. The arbitration field has two subfields: the identifier contains 11 bits and 1 bit for the RTR field (remote transmission request). The identifier controls the messages' priority. Control field is a combination of identifier extension (IDE) (1 bit), reserved (1 bit), and data length code (DLC) (4 bits). Data field (0 to 8 bytes) contains 8 data fields. Check field (16 bits) is divided into cyclic redundancy check (15 bits) and delimiter (DEL) (1 bit). Furthermore, ACK field (2 bits) is split between acknowledgement (1 bit) and delimiter (DEL) (1 bit). Lastly, the CAN bus message frames

DOI: 10.1201/9781003610908-3

TABLE 3.1 The CAN bus message frame standard

Start of frame (SOF) *(1 bit)*	Arbitration field *(12 bits)*		Control field *(6 bits)*			Data field *(0 to 8 bytes)*			Check field *(16 bits)*		ACK field *(2bits)*		End of frame *(7 bits)*	Inter frame space *(3 bits)*
	ID *(11 bits)*	RTR *(1 bit)*	IDE *(1 bit)*	Reserved *(1 bit)*	DLC *(6 bits)*	*Data*			CRC *(15 bits)*	DEL *(1 bit)*	ACK *(1 bit)*	DEL *(1 bit)*		
						0	. . .	*7*						

end with two fields, end of frame (EOF) (7 bits) and inter frame space (IFS) (3 bits). Table 3.1 depicts the CAN bus message frame standard [44].

The SAE J1939 protocol mandates a certain format for the identifier of CAN messages. The ID may be 11 bits in length or 29 bits in the expanded format. All available evidence and John Deere specifications point to the enhanced 29 bit format being in use here [45].

Bit numbers are labelled "CAN 29 BIT ID POSITION" as shown in Table 3.2. Each field's breakdown is as follows:

- Priority (28–26) determines arbitration priority, 0 being the highest and 7 being the lowest priority.
- Extended Data Page (EDP) (25): used in combination with DP to specify different message definitions.
- Data Page (24): used with EDP to determine message definitions.
- PDU Format (23–16): defines the parameter group to which the message belongs; indicates the kind of data being sent.
- PDU Specific (15–8): the address of the device to which the message will be sent.
- Source Address (7–0): is the device's address that is the message's original sender.

CAN bus is typically made to ensure there is dependable communication in autonomous vehicles [46]. As an illustration, the CAN network uses the carrier sense multiple access with collision detection protocol, which enables nodes to intercept unencrypted data sent over the network by hackers. Furthermore, the lack of security measures like user authentication and message encryption makes the ECUs in the CAN bus vulnerable to cyber-attacks [47]. These factors make it necessary to devise security mechanisms to safeguard the CAN bus [48]. In-vehicle intrusion detection has garnered increasing attention and has been studied in a variety of academic fields. CAN bus security has

TABLE 3.2 The format of the identifier of CAN messages [41]

CAN EXTENDED FRAME FORMAT	SOF	IDENTIFIER 11 BITS											SRR	IDE	IDENTIFIER EXTENSION 18 BITS																		RTR
J1939 FRAME FORMAT	SOF	PRIORITY			EDP	DP	PDU FORMAT (PF) 6 BITS (MSB)						SRR	IDE	PF (CONT.)		PDU SPECIFIC (PS) (DESTINATION ADDRESS. GROUP EXT. OR PROPRIETARY)								SOURCE ADDRESS								RTR
		3	2	1			8	7	6	5	4	3			2	1	8	7	6	5	4	3	2	1	8	7	6	5	4	3	2	1	
J1939 FRAME BIT POSITION	1	2	3	4	5	6	7	8	9	10	11	12	13	14	15	16	17	18	19	20	21	22	23	24	25	26	27	28	29	30	31	32	33
CAN 29 BIT ID POSITION		28	27	26	25	24	23	22	21	20	19	18			17	16	15	14	13	12	11	10	9	8	7	6	5	4	3	2	1	0	

attracted researchers' attention due to vehicle network weaknesses. According to experts, most attacks targeting modern vehicles occur through the CAN bus [49]. Several studies have presented approaches to detecting attacks on the CAN bus. Research has suggested detecting the attack based real-time information [50, 51]. Meanwhile, other studies concentrated on a different approach by examining the if dummy packets have been injected and/or missing packets [52, 53]. All these studies have helped to mitigate the CAN bus vulnerabilities but presented some challenges.

3.2 SEVERITY OF PROBLEM

The increase in the number of components in the vehicle led to certain problems in the increased communication demand between these components. As a result, the CAN bus protocol was designed for the purpose of regulating the communication between these components. Security issues were not considered when developing the CAN bus protocol. With the great increase in the number of cars connected to the Internet, these problems have raised security concerns. Security professionals have stated that this protocol breaches confidentiality, integrity, and availability [43–53]. Confidentiality ensures that data is transmitted in an encrypted form and can only be viewed by the authorised entity. Integrity ensures that the data transmitted through the CAN bus protocol has not been tampered with or modified. Availability refers to as ensuring continuity and uninterrupted data flow.

Confidentiality breaches originate from the lack of data encryption in the CAN bus protocol since encryption can cause problems in delaying data arrival resulting in wrong decisions by the AVs. Integrity breaches are due to the CAN bus protocol's lack of authentication. Although the CRC field in the CAN messages framework can mitigate this problem, it shows that the sender of the message was not verified, which raises concerns about whether the attacker sent this packet or not. Availability issues result from depending on the message priority feature of the CAN bus protocol. A DoS attack may cause the network to disconnect, as the nature of this attack is to send high-priority messages, preventing other ECUs from communicating.

Moreover, data privacy issues arose because the data is one of the most important assets. In their research, Chandwani et al. [54] classified data into three categories: driver behaviour data, vehicle safety data, and vehicle security data. Protecting all this data is very important, so data privacy in the vehicle must be preserved. The severity of the attack on the CAN bus protocol is measured by the number of permissions the attacker obtained to attack by controlling one of the nodes inside the vehicle [55]. Attacks that target the vehicle and have high priority are more harmful and destructive than attacks through messages of lower priority. Developing fully safe AVs requires improving the quality of threat detection. The CAN bus system has been used to transmit data inside modern vehicles. The data transfer speed is up to 1 megabit per second. Nodes are not marked as masters or followers on the CAN bus, and all nodes are equal. Therefore, the communication between ECUs is arranged in the order of priority messages. High-priority messages will pass through the CAN bus straight away while low-priority messages are delayed. Vulnerabilities in the CAN bus protocol enable the injection of malicious messages into the in-vehicle network. These injected messages are abnormal network behaviours, which were categorised into three types of attacks (DoS attacks, fuzzy attacks, and spoofing attacks) depending on their severity to the AVs network. A DoS attack represents the injected messages with the CAN ID "0000". The most dominant value is "0000". This attack can limit communication between nodes by sending high-priority messages causing delays in low-priority messages. This delay can cause problems when the CAN bus is exposed to a DDoS attack because the attack depends on sending high-priority messages, which may cause a system failure. Fuzzy attack represents the injected messages with completely random CAN ID and DATA values. The risk of this attack is that it does not require reverse engineering and may cause the vehicle to lose functionality and availability. These injected messages could also be high or low-priority CAN ID. Spoofing attack represents the messages with a fake CAN ID. This identifier is likely to be a high-priority message, and the risk is that it is difficult to differentiate between messages because there is no mechanism to authenticate messages on the CAN bus.

3.3 SOLUTIONS IMPLEMENTED ON CAN BUS

Security CAN bus has drawn researchers' attention to find solutions. The solutions that most studies have come up with are related to encryption and authentication [56–59]. Although these solutions have been useful in a network segmentation, their effectiveness is limited due to complexity of the vehicle systems. ECUs do not have the computational power to perform complex tasks; these solutions require time and space. The intrusion detection systems can help to solve this task with minimal costs in time and space.

Intrusion detection systems can provide effective protection against attacks that other security attack detection systems may not be able to detect.

Several studies have catagorised the intrusion detection systems into four main classes: signature-based IDS, specification-based IDS, anomaly-based IDS, and hybrid-based IDS. Signature-based IDS relies on previous information to determine the nature of the attack already known through the signature [60, 61]. Specification-based IDS is an approach using data traffic specifications to identify normal behaviour of the traffic, and this approach can detect both known and unknown attacks on the network [62, 63]. Anomaly-based IDS is an approach that does not rely on prior information to detect a network attack. This approach depends on the packet's frequency, messages content, or other features [64, 65]. Anomaly-based IDS includes two primary phases: a training phase to describe typical CAN bus traffic behaviour and an execution phase to compare real-time traffic with previous information to find abnormalities. Finally, hybrid IDS utilises a hybrid approach of different intrusion detection techniques to detect abnormal behaviours [66, 67].

Anomaly-based IDS has two subcategories: frequency-based IDS and ML-based IDS. The former focuses on the time frequency to analyse CAN messages sent over the bus. This approach was implemented in [65, 68] by examining the arrival time of messages and comparing them with the time of the previous message, the researchers were able to detect known and unknown threats in the CAN network. The latter is ML-based IDS, which enables supervised and unsupervised learning to detect threats on the CAN bus. Consequently, this approach is the core of the solution to our study, as machine learning-based intrusion detection systems have proven effective in many different systems.

3.4 MACHINE LEARNING AND INTRUSION DETECTION SYSTEM

Machine learning plays an essential role in protecting autonomous vehicles from cyber-attacks. The transport industry anticipates that ML is the future of autonomous vehicles because it can rapidly detect and prevent cyber threats [69]. Several studies have used ML to examine its ability to detect attacks in various areas [70–73]. ML is categorised into three techniques, namely, supervised, unsupervised, and semi-supervised learning (also known as reinforcement learning) [74, 75]. Supervised learning is a form of a machine learning technique in which machines learn from labelled data. Supervised learning is categorised into classification and regression. Unsupervised learning analyses and clusters unlabelled datasets using machine learning methods. These algorithms find hidden data patterns without human interaction. Its capacity to find similarities and contrasts makes it perfect for exploratory data analysis, cross-selling, consumer segmentation, and picture identification. Semi-supervised learning is a combination of supervised and unsupervised learning. Several new forms of learning such as deep learning, transfer learning, and federated learning have emerged due to refinements in the functionality of the three primary categories. Next, we describe the literature review that has been done on ML techniques in in-vehicle network security and other fields.

3.4.1 ML-Based IDS for Securing CAN Bus

Machine learning can play important role in developing cybersecurity solutions based on the log files collected from the cyber-attacks. In a study published in 2019, Zolanvari et al. [72] compared several ML algorithms to detect cyber-attacks in water storage systems. The results showed the SVM had an accuracy of 85%. A study by Ahmed Khan et al. [71] has shown that the k-nearest neighbour (KNN) can be used in detecting cyber-attacks in a gas pipeline, and the model's accuracy reached more than 91%. Similarly, a cyber-attack was detected using the deep neural networks (DNN) algorithm on the power system dataset by [70]. In 2019 Yan et al. [73] used the extreme learning machine (ELM) method to detect threats for securing cyber-physical systems. The results of the aforementioned studies show that ML can be used in different fields to predict known and unknown cyber-attacks.

In terms of the AV application, machine learning has the ability to detect an attack on a CAN bus network [76, 77]. Two studies [76, 77] explored the CAN bus system, identified security risks, and discussed their solutions. In Chowdhury et al.'s [78] research, the authors employ global positioning system (GPS) data to identify drivers using the random forest approach, and their work achieved an accuracy of 82%. The study described in [79] illustrates many types of driver identification characteristics in which the authors gather trip-based data to verify a driver. Traditional machine learning techniques such as SVM, naïve Bayes, and random forest are used to obtain 88% accuracy. Effective IDS using an SVM for monitoring CAN traffic presented by Avatefipour et al. [80]. Their experimental findings show that the proposed model has an accuracy of more than 90%. They utilised open datasets for intrusion detection in CAN bus traffic to ensure the model remained effective. An enhanced SVM-based IDS model was presented by Al-Saud et al. [81]. The model achieved high performance and resilience against just DoS attacks. Similarly, Alshammari et al. [76] proposed two ML algorithms to classify threats to the AV system, and, subsequently, the accuracy of SVM and KNN for detecting fuzzy and DoS attacks reached 96%.

Xiao et al. [82] proposed an RNN-based algorithm for the CAN bus network intrusion detection system. When compared to the LSTM and generative adversarial network (GAN) models, the experimental results reach more than 95% utilising appropriate hyper-parameters. Martìnez et al. [83] proposed an accurate, personalised driving assistance system using 21 unique features such as different vehicle features' speed, distance, direction, pressure, etc. Extreme learning machine, a novel ML approach used in this research, achieves 75% accuracy for 11 drivers, 88% for 5 drivers, and 90% for 3 drivers.

In conclusion, in-vehicle intrusion detection is a growing area of research in many different disciplines. The CAN bus protocol employs intrusion detection to monitor and identify any abnormal communication between ECUs by using traditional machine learning (TML) techniques [69, 84]. Due to the rapid development of in-vehicle networks and rising critical threats, TML-based IDS must be updated to meet the current environment's security requirements.

3.4.2 Deep Learning-Based IDS for Securing CAN Bus

Deep learning, a subset of machine learning, differs from traditional ML methods as it does not necessitate feature engineering. Instead, DL learns data patterns through self-optimising algorithms [85]. Raw data can be directly used in DL algorithms for regression, classification, and decision-making without pre-processing. Additionally, DL operates in supervised, unsupervised, or reinforcement learning settings [86]. Due to its ability to learn patterns that ML cannot, DL is increasingly employed in vehicular networks [68], offering solutions to diverse security challenges in automotive networks.

DL is crucial for in-vehicle communications as it addresses the learning problem. McMahan et al. [87] outlined a practical deep learning approach based on an iterative model, averaging across five different model designs and four datasets through comprehensive empirical evaluation. The results demonstrated the method's flexibility for unbalanced and incongruent distributions with informally, identically distributed (IID) data characterising this scenario. A 2020 study combined convolutional neural network (CNN) and gated recurrent units (GRU) for detecting cyber-attacks in IoT settings [88].

Regarding AV security, Zhu et al. [89] proposed a DL-based technique using LSTM-based intrusion detection. They targeted CAN through spoofing, replay, and flooding attacks. To overcome LSTM's high computation time, they suggested a mobile edge-assisted multi-task model. This model demonstrated over 80% accuracy and 0.61 ms latency. Hossain et al. [90] presented an LSTM-NN-based IDS, asserting that IDS could identify DoS, fuzzing, and spoofing attacks on the CAN bus network. Song et al. [91] developed a deep convolutional neural network (DCNN) model called Inception-ResNet, creating an IDS to detect DoS, fuzzing, gear, and radiation portal monitors (RPM) attacks in real-time in-vehicle systems. After training the CNN classifier, real CAN messages are inputted to identify suspicious messages. Despite achieving a detection rate of over 80% and a low error rate, the model's computational cost and memory usage were not effective. Further research is needed to examine the efficiency of sophisticated cyber-attacks.

A DL model developed by [92] is a cloud-based IDS for in-vehicle networks that investigates various attacks, such as DoS, command injection, and malware. The model achieved an accuracy rate exceeding 86%, prompting further research to improve detection rates, particularly for these attacks. Lokman et al. [92] proposed a deep learning-based IDS for in-vehicle networks, with a 91% detection rate compared to other auto-encoder variants. Further investigation is necessary to demonstrate the IDS's effectiveness against a broader range of cyber-attacks. Seo et al. [93] developed a DL-based intrusion detection system to monitor CAN bus networks for DDoS, RPM, gear, and fuzzy attacks. Utilising only CAN bus data for training, the model could differentiate between normal and unknown messages, recognising all four attacks with 95% accuracy. Zhang et al. [94] proposed a deep learning algorithm-based intrusion detection system for in-vehicle networks, achieving detection accuracy between 97.0% and 98.0%. Despite its performance, the model could only properly identify two attacks. The results were analysed in a simulated environment, warranting further investigation.

In a particular study [68], the authors proposed an intrusion detection system for in-vehicle networks that is rooted in deep neural network principles. Upon acquiring CAN bus data for training, feature vectors were integrated into a probabilistic model. The DNN then ascertained the likelihood of a given packet being either harmful or safe. The authors implemented unsupervised pre-training of a deep belief network (DBN) to fine-tune the parameters, enhancing the accuracy of detection. In the realm of CAN network security, Lin et al. [95] devised a deep learning-based intrusion detection system that specifically pinpoints three categories of attacks. During the training phase, a deep denoising auto-encoder, which incorporates a feature extraction methodology, is employed to train the model. Yang et al. [96] proposed an intrusion detection system that utilises a recurrent neural network. The introduced model has a high success rate in identifying spoofing attacks within the CAN bus network, indicating the need for additional research to detect a variety of cyber-attacks.

In summary, numerous studies have been undertaken to evaluate threat detection using deep learning-based intrusion detection systems. Despite this, these systems have exhibited certain limitations, underscoring the urgent need for more research in this domain.

3.5 RELATED WORK

This section employs the algorithm that has been chosen for this book.

3.5.1 ML Algorithms

3.5.1.1 Support Vector Machine

Support vector machine (SVM) is a powerful machine learning model renowned for its high performance in classification tasks [97, 98], making it a viable tool for detecting cyber-attacks on in-vehicle communication systems in autonomous vehicles. SVM operates by constructing a hyperplane or a set of hyperplanes in a high-dimensional space, which is used for classification, regression, or outlier detection. The primary goal is to create a boundary that maximises the margin between different classes in the training data, thereby allowing for more accurate and robust classification of unseen data [99].

In the context of in-vehicle communication in AVs, SVM can be employed to distinguish between normal traffic patterns and potential threats. This distinction is achieved by using the training data to define an optimal hyperplane that separates the different classes of network traffic. New, unseen data is then classified based on which side of the hyperplane it falls on. SVM has been shown to perform well in scenarios where the number of dimensions is greater than the number of samples [100], making it well-suited for high-dimensional in-vehicle communication data.

The mathematical formulation of SVM is as follows [102, 103]:

$$\min_{w,b,\zeta} \frac{1}{2} \| w^2 \| + C \sum_{i=1}^{n} \zeta_i \tag{1}$$

subject to $y_i\left(w^T \varnothing\left(x_i\right) + b\right) \geq 1 - \zeta_{(i)},\ \zeta_{(i)} \geq 0, \forall\, i = 1,\ldots,n$

where w is the normal vector to the hyperplane, $\varnothing\left(x_i\right)$ are the input vectors, ζ_i refers to the distance to the accurate margin, and it is such that for all i from 1 to n, the value of ζ_i is greater than or equal to zero, y_i are the class labels (+1 for one class, −1 for the other), C is regularisation parameter, and b is the bias.

Figure 3.1 showcases a visual representation of SVM, where the support vectors are the data points closest to the hyperplane, and the goal is to maximise the distance between these points and the hyperplane [98].

While SVM exhibits considerable efficiency, it's not devoid of constraints. The selection of the kernel function has a substantial impact on the model's

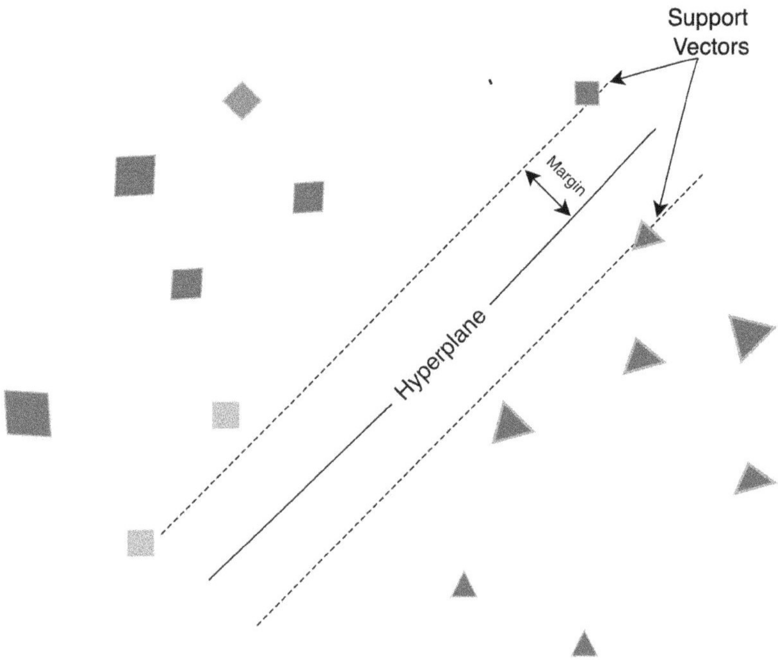

FIGURE 3.1 A schematic depiction of the SVM

performance, but unfortunately, there isn't a one-size-fits-all solution that is optimal for every scenario. Additionally, SVM doesn't inherently offer probability estimates, which could be advantageous in certain applications. Lastly, the SVM can demand significant computational resources, particularly when dealing with large datasets, which could restrict its use in environments with limited resources [103].

Despite these limitations, the ability of SVM to manage high-dimensional data, coupled with its resilience against overfitting, makes it an indispensable asset, particularly in the realm of secure in-vehicle communication within autonomous vehicles.

3.5.1.2 Decision Tree

The decision tree (DT) is a potent statistical instrument employed for data classification, prediction, interpretation, and manipulation [104]. As one of the most efficacious methods in the field of data mining, it finds a wide range of applications in numerous scientific domains [104]. As a supervised learning algorithm, it is visualised as a tree-like model composed of different nodes, namely root nodes, internal nodes, and terminal or leaf nodes [104].

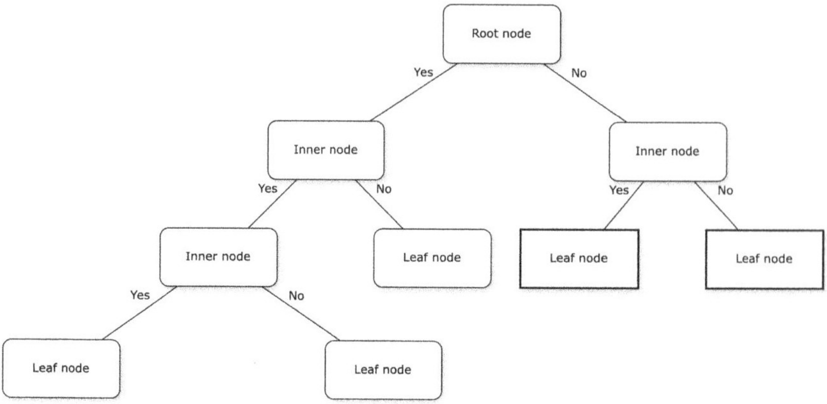

FIGURE 3.2 An example of a decision tree

Root nodes are the decision-making points that segregate records into diverse subsets, embodying the various choices [104]. Internal nodes contribute further to the tree's division, generating either new internal nodes or terminal nodes. Terminal or leaf nodes signify the final decision within the DT [104]. An example of a decision tree structure is represented in Figure 3.2. DT is adept at efficiently handling vast and intricate datasets and simplifying their complexity [105].

To relate this to the context of detecting attacks on in-vehicle communication in autonomous vehicles, consider how a decision tree might be employed. The tree's branches could represent different properties or features of the network traffic, such as message identifier, payload size, and time intervals between messages. These features can help differentiate normal operation from potential cyber-attacks. Each leaf node of the tree could then represent a decision—is this normal network traffic or a potential cyber-attack? By training the decision tree on known examples of both normal operation and cyber-attacks, it can learn to make accurate decisions when presented with new, unknown network traffic data. However, to improve the detection rate and handle large datasets, the decision tree can be incorporated with other machine learning models or techniques [104].

3.5.1.3 Random Forest

Random forest (RF), an extension of the decision tree model [106], serves as an influential mechanism for identifying cyber threats within the in-vehicle communication system of autonomous vehicles. This model operates through the construction of multiple decision trees, each one uniquely generated from random subsets of the original training dataset [106]. Consequently, the resulting forest

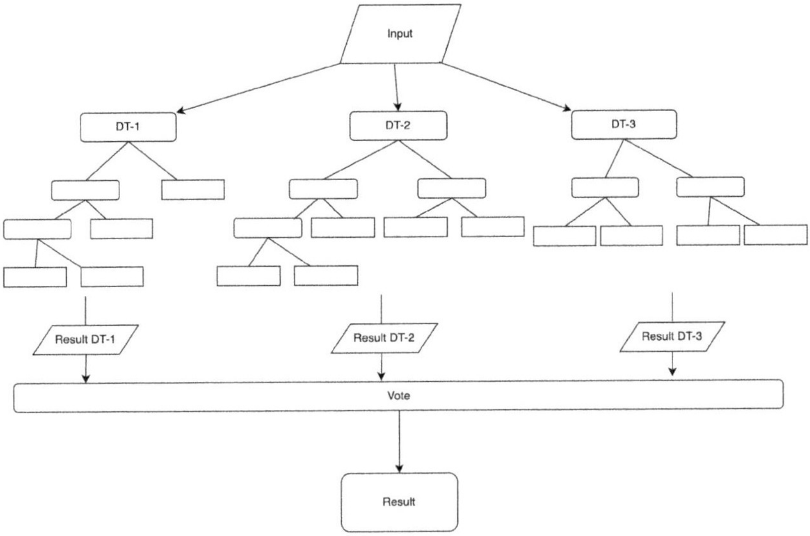

FIGURE 3.3 An example of the RF model

comprises trees that are distinct from one another, thereby reducing the risk of overfitting and noise that typically plague single decision tree models [106].

In the context of cyber-attack detection, each decision tree within the RF model evaluates different aspects of the AV communication data, offering a comprehensive approach to detecting anomalous patterns that could signal potential threats. After each tree has made its prediction, these outcomes are aggregated, and the most frequently occurring prediction is selected as the final classification. This "majority voting" system ensures that the RF model's overall decision is robust against potential errors or anomalies in individual trees' predictions [106].

Figure 3.3 provides a visual representation of this random forest model. It is essential to note that RF's strength lies in its ability to maintain the simplicity of individual decision trees, while its ensemble nature dramatically increases the effectiveness and reliability of the cyber threat detection process in AV communication systems. By adopting such a model, the resilience and security of in-vehicle communication in AVs can be significantly improved.

3.5.1.4 K-Nearest Neighbours

The k-nearest neighbours (KNN) is a robust supervised machine learning technique used for classification, regression, and, crucially, outlier identification [107], making it apt for detecting attacks on in-vehicle communication in AVs.

This technique is favoured for its simplicity in execution, its ability to handle complex tasks, and its time-efficiency [107].

KNN operates by predicting the appropriate classification for test data through the calculation of the distance between the test data and all points in the training set [99]. The KNN algorithm is unique due to its non-parametric and instance-based learning attributes. Non-parametric implies that the algorithm does not depend on predefined training parameters; instead, it retains the training data and leverages it during the classification process of the test point [107]. This characteristic contributes to KNN's high performance in machine learning tasks.

Furthermore, KNN's effectiveness is influenced by the distribution of training points, which is determined by the measure of similarity between data points [107]. This feature is particularly useful in the context of AVs, where data distribution could reflect different driving conditions, vehicle statuses, or potential cybersecurity threats. Figure 3.4 shows an example of KNN [107].

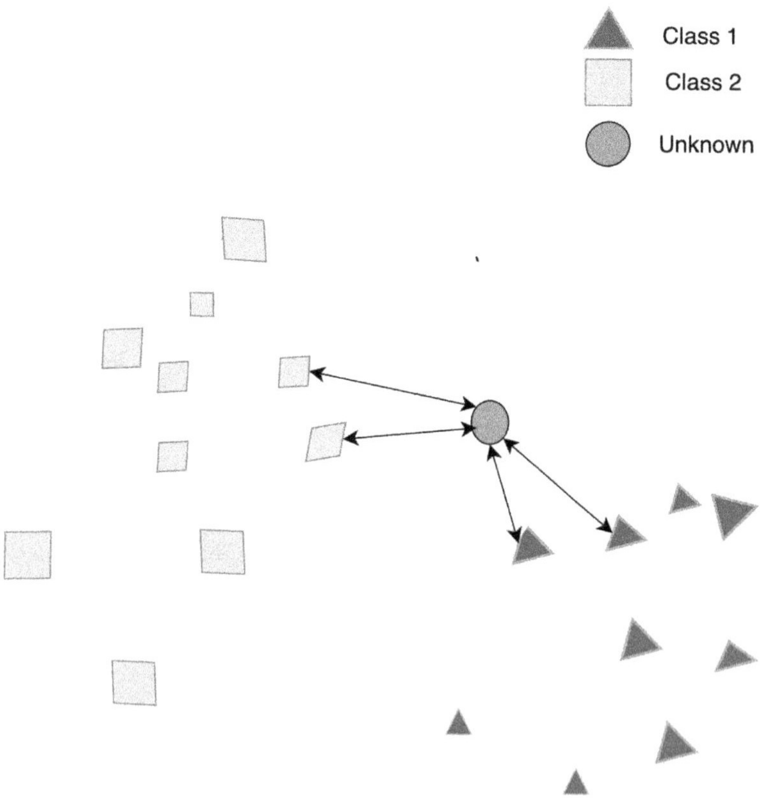

FIGURE 3.4 An example of KNN

To locate the nearest neighbours to a test point—an essential step in detecting anomalies or potential attacks—the Euclidean distance equation is employed as follows [108]:

$$d\left(\chi_i, \chi_j\right) = \sqrt{\sum_{r-1}^{n} (\alpha_r(\chi_i) - \alpha_r(\chi_j))^2} \tag{2}$$

3.5.1.5 *Naïve Bayes*

The naïve Bayes method is a probabilistic classifier rooted in the simple Bayes theorem [109], which is particularly useful in detecting attacks on in-vehicle communication systems in AVs. This technique strives to estimate the probability of each feature occurring within each class, ultimately returning the class with the highest probability. The Bayes theorem equation is represented as follows [109]:

$$P(A \mid B) = \frac{P(B \mid A)P\left(A\right)}{P\left(B\right)} \tag{3}$$

The model proves effective due to the relative ease of calculating probabilities. It is referred to as "naïve" because it assumes that each parameter is independent of the others. Despite this simplification, the naïve Bayes classifier often achieves accuracy comparable to more complex models [109].

In the context of in-vehicle communication in AVs, the naïve Bayes method can be employed to identify anomalous patterns or potential cyber-attacks. By analysing the probabilities of various communication patterns, the classifier can detect unusual activities that might be indicative of an attack. This enables the rapid identification of potential threats and helps safeguard the vehicle's communication system from malicious intrusions.

3.5.2 DL Algorithms

3.5.2.1 *Neural Network*

Neural networks (NNs) are a widely used deep learning approach, known for their superior performance in pattern recognition compared to SVMs [110]. Inspired by the human brain, these networks consist of interconnected algorithms, or neurons, that aim to identify hidden associations within datasets. NNs are used in the context of AVs to analyse sensor data, anticipate vehicle behaviour, and identify abnormalities that may suggest assaults on in-vehicle communication systems.

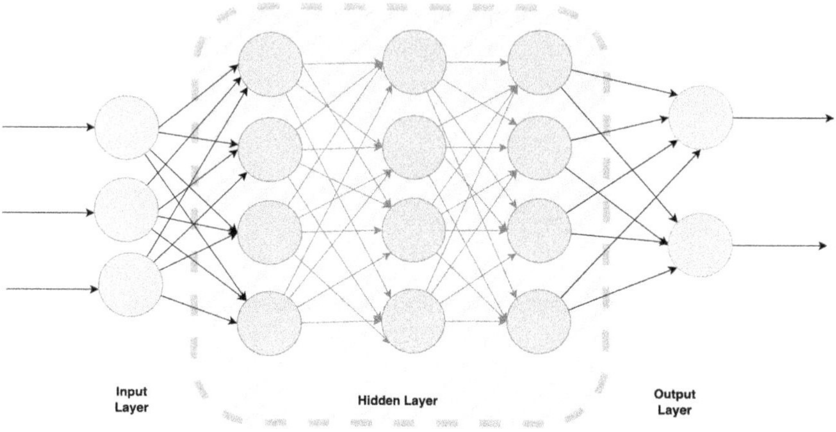

FIGURE 3.5 A neural network architecture

There are typically three main layers in a neural network model: (i) the input layer, which contains the input feature vector; (ii) the output layer, which displays outcomes; and (iii) the hidden layer, which lies between the input and output layers and contains neurons connected to both [110]. Figure 3.5 illustrates the feed-forward neural network architecture, a common type of NN.

The three key constituents of artificial neural networks are the architecture, input and activation functions, and the weight of the input connections. While the network design and functionalities remain consistent throughout training, the weight values critically affect the NN's performance. During training, weights are adjusted to achieve a desired output [110].

One limitation of NNs is their "black box" nature, which makes it challenging to interpret their decision-making processes. However, despite this limitation, their ability to process complex feature data, particularly in detecting anomalies in in-vehicle communication, justifies their adoption as an essential tool in AV security.

3.5.2.2 Convolutional Neural Network

Convolutional neural networks (CNNs) have attracted considerable interest in the field of autonomous vehicles, predominantly due to their high performance on multi-dimensional data, which makes them highly effective at detecting anomalies in in-vehicle communication data. As depicted in Figure 3.6 [111, 112], their name is derived from the mathematical convolution operation that they employ across multiple layers of their network architecture.

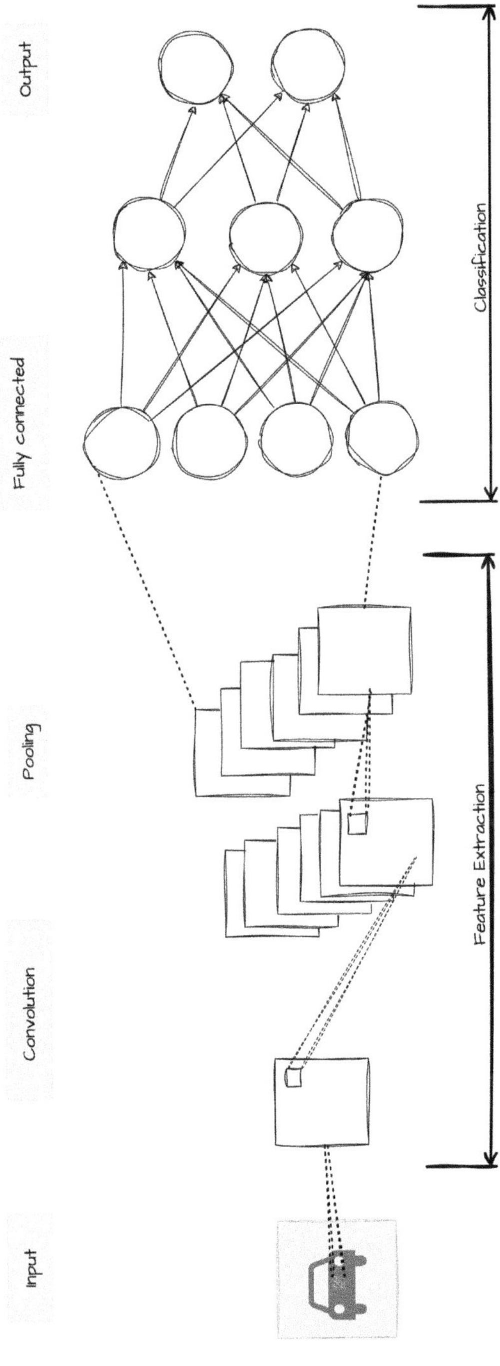

FIGURE 3.6 The architecture of CNN

CNNs are versatile, employing both supervised and unsupervised learning techniques, which makes them highly adaptable for intrusion detection systems (IDS) in AVs, even when dealing with unlabelled data. Their architecture is especially well-suited for processing and interpreting visual data, such as images from the plethora of cameras present in AVs. This ability is crucial in detecting suspicious activities that could indicate unauthorised physical tampering with the vehicle or cyber-attacks targeting the in-vehicle communication system [111].

One of the distinguishing features of CNNs is their weight-sharing and pooling operations, which enable them to efficiently handle high-dimensional data with fewer parameters compared to traditional neural networks. This feature translates into robust training performance and a heightened ability to discern complex patterns within the data.

3.5.2.3 Recurrent Neural Network

Recurrent neural networks (RNNs) are a class of deep learning networks designed for processing sequential data [111], making them particularly useful for detecting attacks on in-vehicle communication systems in AVs. RNNs are distinguished by a feedback loop structure that enables them to maintain state information over time, as the most recent output is dependent on both the current input and previous output [111, 113]. This unique feature enables RNNs to analyse sequences of telemetric data from AVs and identify patterns that may signify potential cyber-attacks. Figure 3.7 showcases the architecture of an RNN.

In the context of in-vehicle communication security, RNNs play a critical role in detecting abnormal patterns in sequential data, which may indicate cyber-attacks on AV systems. Although they may not be suitable for some applications, such as understanding frames in videos or text blocks (where convolutional neural networks might be more appropriate), RNNs remain an essential tool for processing sequence data and ensuring the security of in-vehicle communication in AVs.

While RNNs excel at handling time-dependent data, they often face challenges when dealing with long sequences, due to issues such as vanishing and exploding gradients. These issues can hinder the network's capacity for effective data-driven learning. Consequently, more advanced variants such as long short-term memory (LSTM) networks have emerged to circumvent these restrictions.

3.5.2.4 Long Short-Term Memory

Long short-term memory, a sophisticated variant of recurrent neural networks (RNNs), has emerged as a vital tool for in-vehicle communication security in

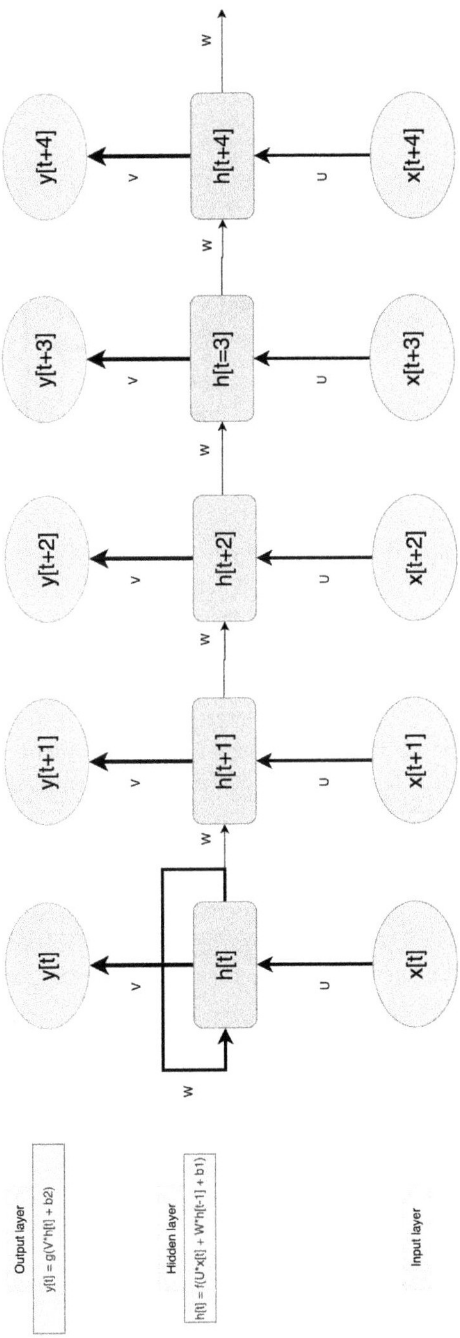

FIGURE 3.7 The RNN architecture

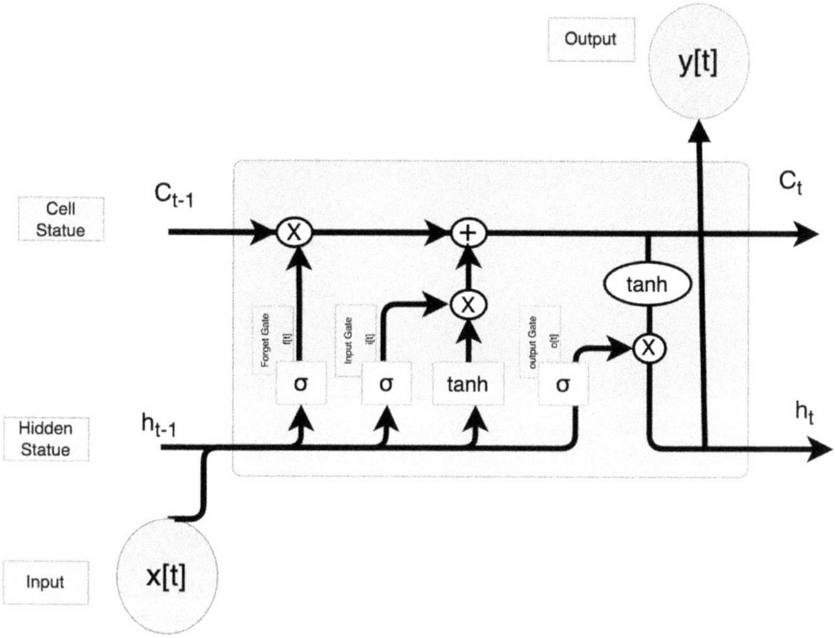

FIGURE 3.8 The internal architecture of LTSM

AVs. Its strength lies in its ability to process extended sequences of time-series data [114, 115], a critical feature when dealing with streams of sensor data or intricate vehicle routing information.

LSTM networks tackle two critical issues often associated with RNNs—the vanishing and exploding gradient problems. These problems can impair the learning process and predictive performance of the network. The LSTM's unique internal architecture, depicted in Figure 3.8, enables it to circumvent these issues, thereby ensuring more effective learning from long sequences of data [116].

However, this enhanced capability comes with a caveat—LSTM networks are more computationally demanding due to their complex architecture. This demand can potentially limit their deployment in resource-constrained environments. Despite this, the rapid advancements in computational power continue to broaden the scope of LSTM applications in AVs.

In the context of in-vehicle communication security, LSTM can be pivotal in detecting anomalous patterns in data sequences, which may signify potential cyber-attacks. Consequently, it plays a crucial role in safeguarding AVs against security threats and fostering safer, more reliable autonomous transportation systems.

Research Design 4

4.1 PROPOSED SOLUTION

The development of efficient intrusion detection systems will reduce the severity of this problem. Depending on the nature of the data transmitted on the CAN bus, the focus is on CAN ID since it contains information that will determine the importance of the message; and secondly, it will affect the flow of data sent in the CAN network. We proposed adding a step after the pre-processing phase of the data and before the training phase. This step distinguishes between high-priority and low-priority messages. High-priority messages will be sent to deep learning algorithms since they are more accurate and efficient. To maintain data flow and ensure no collisions occur, all low-priority messages will be sent to machine learning algorithms as they offer high accuracy and speed in prediction. According to the structure of the CAN bus message frame standard, the feature responsible for setting priority is CAN ID. The lower the ID number, then the higher will be its priority.

Specifically, according to the format of the identifier of CAN messages, the arbitration priority was determined, with 0 being the highest and 7 the lowest priority. So an identifier with 0 is a top priority on the network. Theoretically, a threshold has been set at 1 to demonstrate the priority of messages and to evaluate how well the model performs, whereas the CAN ID sent over the CAN bus is in hexadecimal format; it should be converted to decimal values. The CAN ID will undergo a conditional statement (if CAN ID is less than 1, the message will be passed to deep learning algorithms, otherwise, it will be passed to machine learning algorithms). Figure 4.1 illustrates the steps for implementing the proposed model. This will improve the effectiveness of the model for detecting threats in the CAN network, in addition to accelerating the prediction process in DL and ML algorithms.

DOI: 10.1201/9781003610908-4

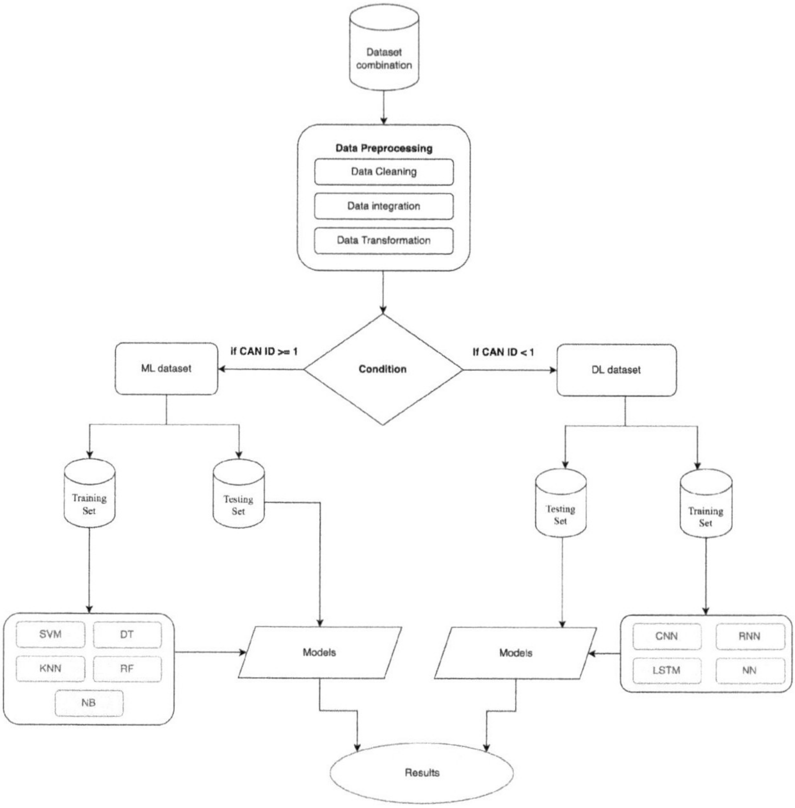

FIGURE 4.1 The proposed IDS framework

4.2 EXPERIMENT

4.2.1 Dataset Description

The dataset called "car-hacking dataset" proposed by [93] contains Hyundai's YF Sonata CAN network traffic, including both normal and attack messages. Datasets were generated by recording CAN traffic from a real vehicle's OBD-II port when message injection attacks took place. The dataset was generated via two methods. The first data set was collected under non-attack conditions, whereas the second dataset was gathered from the vehicle experiencing attacks on its internal networks. The car-hacking datasets include four types of attack in CSV files, which include DoS attack, fuzzy attack, spoofing the drive gear, and spoofing the RPM. All the CSV files have the same features: Timestamp, CAN ID, DLC, Data Field (0–7), and Flag. All datasets were integrated into one CSV file using a Python script, as shown in Figure 4.2. The Timestamp feature indicates the time in seconds that was captured (s). The CAN ID identifies CAN messages and represents their priority in hexadecimal format. Smaller CAN ID values suggest higher priority messages. DLC denotes the number of bytes, from 0 to 8, and these values shift depending on the vehicle type. The Data feature holds the data to be transmitted between the nodes. Lastly, the Flag feature has two numeric values, namely 0 and 1, which represent normal and attack, respectively.

The target distribution of normal and abnormal messages in the dataset is shown in Figure 4.3. It is very clear that abnormal messages are fewer than

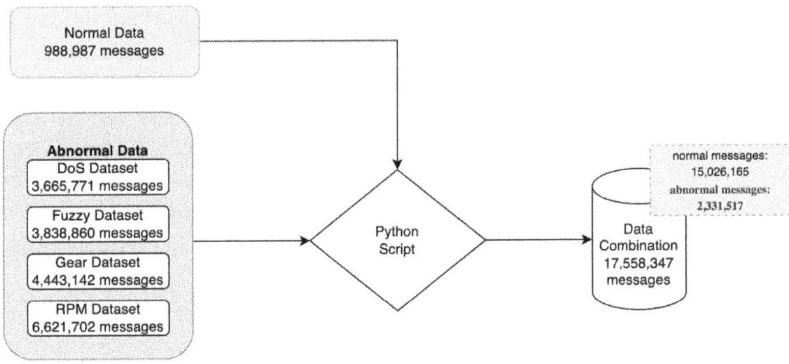

FIGURE 4.2 The combined datasets

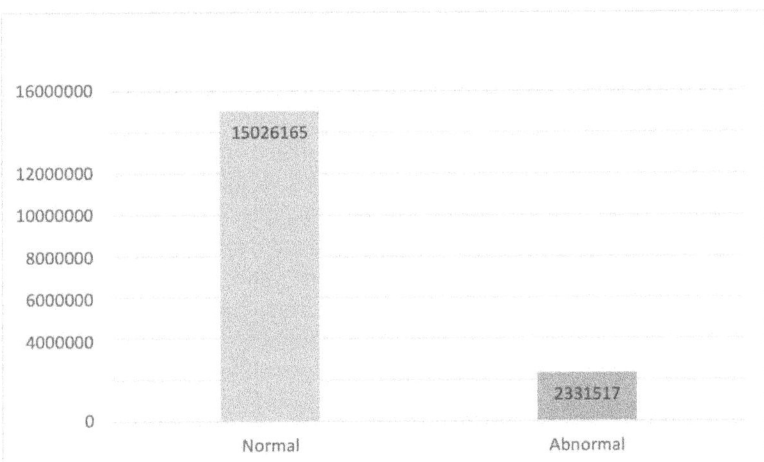

FIGURE 4.3 Distribution of the normality of the dataset

normal messages. However, if we train our model on this dataset, it will be significantly biased towards normal messages. In the data preparation step, we will undertake data balancing to counteract the model's inherent bias.

4.2.2 Dataset Preparation

Dataset preparation is one of the most crucial and challenging aspects of any machine learning or deep learning activity. The quality of the dataset impacts the model's performance and training process, so we need to ensure that dataset is suitable, has no missing values or/and outliers, or is not in a format that the model cannot understand. In order to develop a high-performance model that would accurately predict respective classes and work well on the untested new input dataset, the dataset must be cleaned, prepared, and transformed before employing any method. In general, addressing missing values, eliminating unnecessary columns, looking for any independent features, turning all of the category columns into numerical columns, and eliminating outliers are all aspects of the data preparation process. In the proposed system, we have executed data cleaning and data transformation on the combined dataset that we get from merging all the attacks CSVs and the normal run data text file.

4.2.2.1 Data Pre-Processing

Due to the big size of the dataset, which has 17,558,347 instances and it includes a significant amount of duplicate and missing data. All the missing data and duplicate values were identified through exploratory data analysis and screening. The essential steps for data prepossessing are described in more detail in this subsection.

Firstly, we noted that the data that had less than 8 bytes contained only missing values. When we looked for the source of these missing values by filtering the data that had missing values, we discovered that all the instances were normal messages. This was the case when we filtered only the data that had missing values. Since our dataset already includes many normal messages, we eliminated missing and duplicate values since they do not affect the model's performance. Another feature that was removed from the dataset was due to its redundancy of DLC feature, which represents the number of bytes. This feature does not affect performance; the Timestamp feature was also eliminated because it may trigger data overfitting. After that, the dataset was very unbalanced, causing our model to be biased towards normal messages; hence, we included an equal amount of normal messages and attack messages to balance the dataset. Because machine learning and deep learning models can only operate on numerical values, the next step was to turn the non-numerical

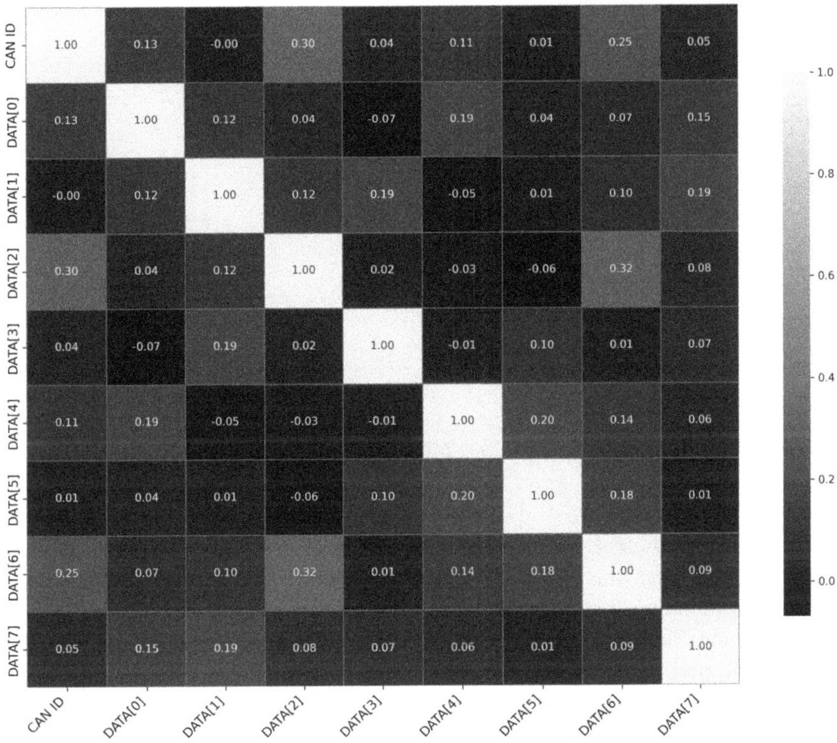

FIGURE 4.4 The correlation between different features

values into numerical ones. The Flag in the dataset contained non-numerical values such as R, which represents normal data, and T, which represents the type of attack (DoS, RPM, gear, and fuzzy). We converted these values into 0 and 1, where 0 denotes the normal messages and 1 stands for attack messages. Next, the hexadecimal values of the CAN ID and all the data values were converted into decimal values via the "*int*" function with a base of 16. Figure 4.4 shows the correlation between the different features after the data-cleaning process.

4.2.2.2 Data Transformation

The dataset contains values with varying scales; certain features are more extreme than others, which might compromise the model's accuracy. For this reason, we have used data transformation or feature scaling to the dataset to enhance the model's accuracy. Feature scaling is a method for normalising the

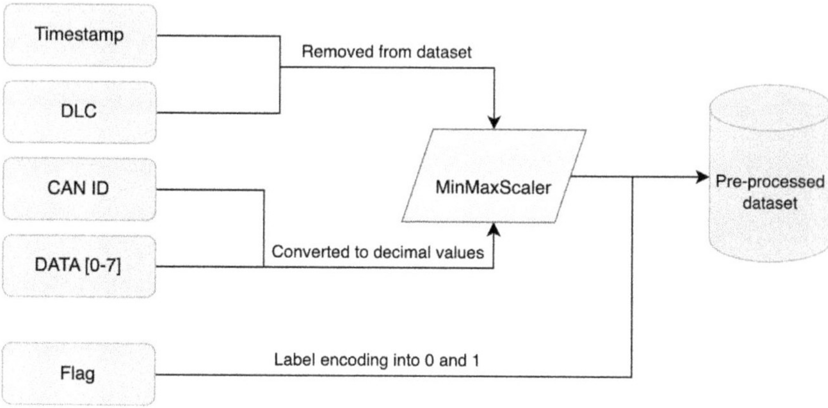

FIGURE 4.5 The preparation phase process

variety of independent variables or data features. Typically, it is done during the data pre-processing step and is frequently referred to as data normalisation within the context of data processing. We have re-scaled the feature values within a range between 0 and 1, without affecting the properties of the original data. To do that, we have used a minimum-maximum normalisation equation. This is referred to as Equation (4), which is written as follows:

$$X' = \frac{x - \min(x)}{\max(x) - \min(x)} \tag{4}$$

The normalised output values are denoted by X', while the original values are denoted by X. The max(x) is the maximum feature values and min(x) stands for the minimum feature values. We undertook this technique by importing MinMaxScaler from the Sklearn library, which is used for scaling down the features in the range. The Flag column in the dataset contains qualitative values "normal and abnormal", we converted it using LabelEncoder fitted so that it became 0 and 1. The total amount of data remaining after the data pre-processing phase amounts to 908,764 rows. Figure 4.5 shows the process that we have executed in the data preparation phase. Following that, our proposed step turns to training the model, as previously explained in Section 4.1.

4.2.3 Training Phase

Following the data pre-processing phase, we have the final cleaned data ready for training. Now the dataset in the training process will be divided into two

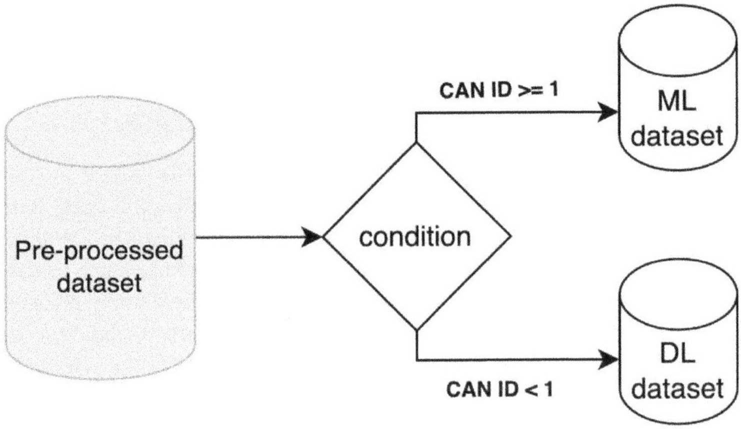

FIGURE 4.6 Splitting data based on its priority

datasets "DL dataset" and "ML dataset". Each dataset will train the model through certain algorithms. Doing this will ensure the efficiency of the training process and speed up the model's work and, subsequently, ensure they can work together in parallel. The first dataset, i.e. "DL dataset", is for high-priority data that will be trained on deep learning algorithms to detect threats accurately; this category contains about 454,289 rows of data. The second dataset, "ML dataset", comprises 454,475 rows of low-priority data, which will be trained on traditional machine learning algorithms. Figure 4.6 shows the process of splitting data based on its priority.

4.2.3.1 Machine Learning-Based Intrusion Detection

After pre-processing the data and applying our proposed solution by sorting the data according to priority, we have 454,475 data values out of a total of 908,764 for the machine learning dataset. We divided the dataset into training and testing sets with a training size of 80% of the total data and a testing size of 20% of the total data with a randomised set of 42 cases to execute the model's training and evaluate its performance. The testing dataset contains 90,895 data values, while the training dataset contains 363,580 data values. This step was done utilising the *train_test_split* with the *scikit_learn* library to split the dataset.

Since our dataset is labelled, we have used several supervised learning algorithms. These algorithms have been selected since they are widely employed in security and have shown excellent performance [117]. The machine learning algorithms used are support vector machine (SVM), random forest classifier, decision tree classifier, k-nearest neighbours, and naïve Bayes classifier.

4.2.3.2 Deep Learning-Based Intrusion Detection

To showcase models to exhibit great accuracy and performance on the test dataset with machine learning algorithms, we also tested the deep learning models to see how they work with the given dataset. We have 454,289 data values out of a total of 908,764 for the deep learning dataset after pre-processing the data and applying our proposed solution by sorting the data by priority and the attacks' severity. This dataset is further divided into two datasets: firstly, 80% of the data for the training set and it contains 363,431 of the selected datasets for deep learning algorithms; and secondly, 20% of the data for the testing consisting of 90,858 data values.

Deep learning models like neural networks, long short-term memory, recurrent neural networks, and convolution neural networks are often used for classifying messages as attack and normal due to their ability to handle sequence data, high-dimensional data, and non-linear relationships. A neural network consists of an input layer, one or more hidden layers, and an output layer. Each node, or artificial neuron, is connected to others and has a weight and threshold that goes along with it. If the output exceeds the threshold value of the node, it will be activated and provide data to the next layer. Otherwise, no data is transmitted to the network's next tier. We have used simple neural networks with an input layer with 256 units or neurons, three hidden layers with 128, 64, and 32 units with activation function as the hyperbolic tangent function "*tanh*", and an output layer of 1 unit with an activation function as sigmoid. Since the target is in binary form, "*binary_crossentropy*" is a loss function and "*adam*" (adaptive moment estimation) is an optimiser. The training of the data runs on 10 epochs with 64 batch size; validation data used is the test dataset that we created using splitting the dataset into training and testing sets with an 80:20 ratio. All other deep learning algorithms have the same structure as described for the simple neural network. Getting different models with great accuracy and performance on the test dataset with machine learning algorithms, we tested the deep learning models to see how they work with the given dataset.

Results and Discussion 5

5.1 MODEL EVALUATION METRICS

After selecting the machine learning and deep learning models, the final step in the process is to evaluate the models, using statistical methods, while different metrics are used to evaluate model performance. The Sklearn library is used to calculate different metrics on each model; specifically, these are accuracy, precision, recall, F1-score, sensitivity, and specificity. The performance will be evaluated according for four metrics: true positive (TP), true negative (TN), false positive (FP), and false negative (FN), where TP is the number of correctly detected attack predictions classified as an attack, and TN is the number of correctly detected normal predictions classified as normal. In the meantime, FP stands for the number of detected normal predicted and classified as attacks, while FN is the number of falsely detected attacks predicted and classified as normal.

Accuracy is a derivative of the confusion matrix, which is a metric for evaluating a model's efficiency. Accuracy can be defined mathematically as follows: $TP + TN$.

$$Accuracy = \frac{TP + TN}{TP + TN + FP + FN} \quad (5)$$

Precision is a classification metric that reveals how many are true positive predictions that have been labelled as positive. In other words, it shows a proportion of instances classified as a real attack among all of the cases classified as an attack. Precision can be defined mathematically as follows:

$$Precision = \frac{TP}{TP + FP} \quad (6)$$

DOI: 10.1201/9781003610908-5

Recall represents the cases identified correctly among all positive cases. Mathematically, recall is defined in the following way:

$$Recall = \frac{TP}{TP + \mathrm{FN}} \tag{7}$$

An F1-score indicates the accuracy of the model on a dataset. The F1-score is a method for integrating the model's precision and recall, which is defined as the harmonic mean of precision and recall. The mathematical definition of the F1-score is written here:

$$F1 - score = 2 \times \frac{Precision \times Recall}{Precision + Recall} \tag{8}$$

Sensitivity is the true positive rate (TPR), which means its ability to determine the attack cases correctly. While specificity is the true negative rate (TNR), it is able to determine the normal cases correctly. Sensitivity and specificity can be defined mathematically as follows:

$$Sensitivity = \frac{TP}{TP + \mathrm{FN}} \tag{9}$$

$$Specificity = \frac{T\mathrm{N}}{T\mathrm{N} + \mathrm{FP}} \tag{10}$$

5.2 RESULTS

5.2.1 ML-Based IDS Model Results

The following machine learning algorithms were used on low-priority data due to their ability to deliver high performance and efficiency, characterised by their fast operational speed. We used standard model evaluation metrics to assess the effectiveness of these machine learning algorithms. Table 5.1 illustrates the performance of the algorithms.

The results show that SVM performed well as compared to other ML algorithms we used parameters: C=1.2 and kernel = '*rbf*', and it gave us an accuracy of 99.91%. The precision, recall, and F1-score rates were all 100%. Similarly, KNN showed high performance where the accuracy rate reached 99.82% and a precision rate of 99%. Meanwhile, the recall and F1-score reached 100%. Conversely, the RF algorithm achieved the third best accuracy rate of 97.42% with a precision rate of 94%. Recall rates of 98% and F1-score

TABLE 5.1 The performance of each ML algorithm

MODELS	*ACCURACY*	*PRECISION*	*RECALL*	*F1-SCORE*	*SENSITIVITY*	*SPECIFICITY*
SVM	99.91	100	100	100	0.99	0.99
Random forest	97.42	94	98	96	0.97	0.97
KNN	99.82	99	100	100	0.99	0.99
Decision tree	97.06	93	99	96	0.98	0.96
Naïve Bayes	96.11	92	97	94	0.96	0.95

of more than 96% were achieved. However, RF and DT had a convergent accuracy rate of around 97.42% for the RF algorithm and over 97% for the DT algorithm. The naïve Bayes algorithm has the lowest recall rate at approximately 96%. Considering all performance metrics, we found that the SVM algorithm performs better than the other four TML in classifying normal and attack messages.

5.2.2 DL-Based Model Results

The DL algorithms have been used for intrusion detection classification tasks [82]. Due to their performance in classification challenges, basic neural networks (NN), long short-term memory (LSTM), recurrent neural networks (RNN), and convolution neural networks (CNN) are utilised as deep learning models for determining if a message is an attack or normal. The proposed models showed excellent performance in deep learning algorithms. Table 5.2 summarises the performance results of deep learning algorithms after the data has been divided according to its priority and attacks severity. We employed basic neural networks in the training phase with 256 input units; 128, 64, 32 hidden units with *tanh* activation; and 1 sigmoid output unit. Given that the objective is binary, *binary_crossentropy* is utilised as a loss function, and *adam* serves as an optimiser.

The training dataset contains 10 epochs and 64 batches, while the validation dataset was constructed by dividing the train dataset on an 80:20 ratio. All other deep learning methods have the same structure as the basic neural network. Here NN achieved the highest accuracy rate of 99.96%, followed by the CNN algorithm, which reached 97.58%, while the RNN algorithm was in third place with an accuracy of more than 97.31%. Furthermore, LSTM showed the poorest accuracy of all deep learning algorithms; their performance improved after applying the proposed solution. Finally, considering all performance metrics of the DL models, we reported that the NN algorithm achieved the best performance out of all other DL algorithms.

TABLE 5.2 The performance of each DL algorithm

MODELS	*ACCURACY*	*PRECISION*	*RECALL*	*F1-SCORE*	*SENSITIVITY*	*SPECIFICITY*
NN	99.96	100	100	100	0.99	0.99
LSTM	96.53	96	99	97	0.98	0.92
RNN	97.31	97	99	98	0.98	0.94
CNN	97.58	97	100	98	0.99	0.93

TABLE 5.3 The performance of all selected algorithms before applying the proposed model

MODELS	*ACCURACY*	*PRECISION*	*RECALL*	*F1 SCORE*	*SENSITIVITY*	*SPECIFICITY*
SVM	99.90	100	100	100	0.99	0.99
Random forest	95.96	96	96	96	0.96	0.95
KNN	99.78	100	100	100	0.99	0.99
Decision tree	93.55	91	96	94	0.96	0.90
Naïve Bayes	91.17	90	93	91	0.93	0.89
NN	99.95	100	100	100	0.99	0.99
LSTM	96.31	95	98	96	0.97	0.95
RNN	95.82	93	99	96	0.98	0.92
CNN	94.24	94	94	94	0.94	0.94

5.3 COMPARISON OF THE PROPOSED SOLUTION

It is pertinent to state here that our approach to data processing has achieved the desired goal of improving the accuracy of intrusion detection on the CAN bus. The selected algorithms achieved more accurate results compared to previous studies. By comparing them in our proposed solution, the proposed model achieved high performance in all algorithms. This is in addition to accelerating the intrusion detection process in the CAN system. Table 5.3 shows all the values calculated from various metrics on different models before applying the proposed model.

5.4 DISCUSSION

We proposed a new architecture based on the nature of AV data. The proposed solution is built on supervised learning models that are trained on the dataset that includes four different types of attacks: DoS attacks, fuzzy attacks, drive gear spoofing, and RPM spoofing.

The results of our experiment showed that the proposed model achieved superior performance and speed in detecting threats on the CAN bus network compared to other models. Our proposed model can detect threats based on their severity because it classifies traffic in a CAN bus into abnormal and normal. According to the format of the identifier of CAN messages, messages follow a priority approach and range from 0 to 7, whereby messages of lower value are more important. Furthermore, they have the right to pass through the CAN bus first, while messages with lower priority are delayed.

The proposed model distinguished all high-priority messages and transformed them into deep learning algorithms. The results of the DL algorithms have shown high accuracy and effectiveness in detecting highly severe threats (under the three categories: DoS attacks, fuzzy attacks, and spoofing) that can disrupt the system. The NN algorithm achieved the highest accuracy rate of 99.96%, compared with the other algorithms. Meanwhile, all messages with low priority have been passed to ML algorithms which achieved high-performance results and speed in detecting threats. Two of the five used ML algorithms achieved an accuracy of more than 99%, namely SVM and KNN. The proposed model ensures the continuity of high and low-priority data flow, with no collision, and certainly ensures its security.

It can be conclusively stated that the research queries outlined in the introduction have been thoroughly addressed. The model proposed herein, underpinned by machine learning (ML) and deep learning (DL) algorithms, manifests a potential to bolster the security framework of autonomous vehicles (AVs) by identifying threats with notable accuracy. A meticulous analysis of CAN messages facilitated the discernment of the severity of attacks targeting AVs' internal networks, highlighting "priority in CAN ID" as a salient determinant for both, the targeting of the CAN bus, and the classification of messages. The implementation of this method resulted in a reduction of message waiting time, thereby minimising latency.

The objectives initially outlined have been met through the development of an intrusion detection system (IDS) proficient in identifying attacks on the CAN bus network with remarkable precision and minimal latency. The devised system fortifies the security of the CAN bus network by detecting four distinct types of threats: denial of service (DoS) attacks, fuzzy attacks, gear spoofing, and RPM spoofing. However, all four types of threats were treated as anomalies (abnormal data), further reinforcing the comprehensive nature of our system's threat detection capabilities. Empirical evidence demonstrates that our proposed system can detect attacks with a negligible error rate, thereby enhancing public trust in the security mechanisms of autonomous vehicles (AVs) and potentially accelerating the widespread acceptance and adoption of AVs within the automotive industry.

Conclusions and Future Research 6

6.1 CONCLUSIONS

New security dangers arise as car connectivity is made possible with networks or made more complex over time because communication methods like the CAN network are still insecure and open to intrusion. For this reason, in-vehicle communication systems now require much attention to address automobile cybersecurity. This study proposed a lightweight classification model for intrusion detection for in-vehicle network security using machine learning and deep learning methods. Our proposed method minimises classification errors by utilising a balanced class and a limited number of attributes to speed up intrusion detection. IDS has been made more efficient by focusing on the important data transmitted in the CAN bus network. The models are trained using dataset, and they appropriately categorised each message as an attack or normal with an accuracy of above 99% on the CAN bus dataset. It is noted that three algorithms provide more than 99.5% accuracy, which means that these models will classify intrusion accurately with 0.005% error.

6.2 FUTURE RESEARCH

This study presented a machine learning model that aims to enhance the security of AVs' communication by detecting cyber-attacks using machine learning and deep learning algorithms. However, several avenues for future work can be explored to further advance this area of research.

DOI: 10.1201/9781003610908-6

One potential direction for future work is to optimise the model's accuracy and robustness by incorporating additional data sources and refining the feature selection process. For instance, the model can be trained on larger datasets, including various attack scenarios and network conditions, to improve its ability to detect and prevent cyber-attacks. Additionally, hyperparameter tuning can be applied to enhance the model's performance and generalizability. Secondly, the model's effectiveness and reliability can be further assessed through real-world testing and validation. This can be accomplished by collaborating with AV manufacturers and cybersecurity experts to conduct a rigorous evaluation in simulated and field tests. This is critical to ensuring the model's practical application and utility in real-world settings.

Moreover, integrating the intrusion detection system (IDS) with other cybersecurity measures such as firewalls and encryption protocols can be investigated to provide comprehensive protection for AVs. The research can also explore developing a hybrid approach that integrates traditional and machine learning-based IDS methods. Additionally, the study's findings can be extended to other autonomous systems, such as robots and drones to address cybersecurity issues in the field of robotics. Finally, the model's scalability and applicability can be assessed to determine its potential for deployment in large-scale autonomous systems. The study can investigate the integration of the proposed model with the emerging 5G networks to enhance the security and reliability of autonomous systems.

In conclusion, this study provides a promising approach for enhancing the security of AVs communication using machine learning and deep learning algorithms. However, future research and development are essential to optimise the model's performance and extend its applicability to other autonomous systems such as robots and drones. Nevertheless, the findings of this study have significant implications for the safe and secure deployment of autonomous systems, contributing to the advancement of the field of robotics and cybersecurity.

References

1. Ferber, J. and O. Gutknecht, A meta-model for the analysis and design of organizations in multi-agent systems. In *Proceedings International Conference on Multi Agent Systems (Cat . No. 98EX160)*, 1998. IEEE.
2. Campos-Rodriguez, R., L. Gonzalez-Jimenez, F. Cervantes-Alvarez, F. Amezcua-Garcia, and M. Fernandez-Garcia, Multiagent Systems in Automotive Applications. *Multi-agent Systems*. InTech, Sep. 13, 2017. doi: 10.5772/intechopen.69687.
3. Balaji, P.G. and D. Srinivasan (Eds.), An introduction to multi-agent systems. In *Innovations in multi-agent systems and applications-1*, 2010. Studies in Computational Intekkigence, Vol 310. Springer. pp. 1–27.
4. Fadhil, J.A. and Q.I. Sarhan, Internet of Vehicles (IoV): A survey of challenges and solutions. In *2020 21st International Arab Conference on Information Technology (ACIT)*, 2020. IEEE.
5. Cañedo, J. and A. Skjellum, Using machine learning to secure IoT systems. In *2016 14th Annual Conference on Privacy, Security and Trust (PST)*, 2016.
6. Qureshi, K.N., et al., Internet of vehicles: Key technologies, network model, solutions and challenges with future aspects. *IEEE Transactions on Intelligent Transportation Systems*, 2020. 22(3): pp. 1777–1786.
7. Yang, F., et al., An overview of internet of vehicles. *China Communications*, 2014. 11(10): pp. 1–15.
8. Guo, L., et al., A secure mechanism for big data collection in large scale internet of vehicle. *IEEE Internet of Things Journal*, 2017. 4(2): pp. 601–610.
9. Arooj, A., et al., Big data processing and analysis in internet of vehicles: Architecture, taxonomy, and open research challenges. *Archives of Computational Methods in Engineering*, 2022. 29: pp. 793–829.
10. Milakis, D., et al., Development and transport implications of automated vehicles in the Netherlands: Scenarios for 2030 and 2050. *European Journal of Transport and Infrastructure Research*, 2017. 17(1): pp. 63–85.
11. Texas Instruments. *Introduction to the Controller Area Network (CAN)*; Application Report SLOA101; Texas Instruments: Dallas, TX, USA, 2002; pp. 1–17.
12. Lin, X., et al., GSIS: A secure and privacy-preserving protocol for vehicular communications. *IEEE Transactions on Vehicular Technology*, 2007. 56(6): pp. 3442–3456.
13. Sun, Y., et al., Security and privacy in the Internet of Vehicles. In *2015 International Conference on Identification, Information, and Knowledge in the Internet of Things (IIKI)*, 2015. IEEE.
14. Lokman, S.-F., A.T. Othman, and M.-H. Abu-Bakar, Intrusion detection system for automotive Controller Area Network (CAN) bus system: A review. *EURASIP Journal on Wireless Communications and Networking*, 2019. 2019(1): p. 184.
15. Hasan, K.F., Overall, A., Ansari, K., Ramachandran, G.S., & Jurdak, R. Security, Privacy and Trust: Cognitive Internet of Vehicles. *ArXiv*, 2021. abs/2104.12878.

16. Miftah, E., A. Sayouti, and H. Medromi, Multi-agent systems and its application to control vehicle underwater. *International Journal of Applied Information Systems*, 2015. 9(7): pp. 29–38.
17. Wrona, Z., Buchwald, W., Ganzha, M., Paprzycki, M., Leon, F., Noor, N., & Pal, C.-V. Overview of Software Agent Platforms Available in 2023. *Information*, 2023. 14(6): p. 348. https://doi.org/10.3390/info14060348
18. Ouaissa, M., et al., A secure vehicle to everything (V2X) communication model for intelligent transportation system. In *Computational intelligence in recent communication networks*, 2022. Springer. pp. 83–102.
19. Choy, M.C., D. Srinivasan, and R.L. Cheu, Neural networks for continuous online learning and control. *IEEE Transactions on Neural Networks*, 2006. 17(6): pp. 1511–1531.
20. Choy, M.C., D. Srinivasan, and R.L. Cheu, Cooperative, hybrid agent architecture for real-time traffic signal control. *IEEE Transactions on Systems, Man, and Cybernetics- Part A: Systems and Humans*, 2003. 33(5): pp. 597–607.
21. Lander, S.E., Issues in multiagent design systems. *IEEE Expert*, 1997. 12(2): pp. 18–26.
22. Müller, J.P. and K. Fischer, Application impact of multi-agent systems and technologies: A survey. In *Agent-oriented software engineering*, 2014. Springer.
23. Kober, J., J.A. Bagnell, and J. Peters, Reinforcement learning in robotics: A survey. *The International Journal of Robotics Research*, 2013. 32(11): pp. 1238–1274.
24. Shakshuki, E. and M. Reid, Multi-agent system applications in healthcare: Current technology and future roadmap. *Procedia Computer Science*, 2015. 52: pp. 252–261.
25. Derakhshan, F. and S. Yousefi, A review on the applications of multiagent systems in wireless sensor networks. *International Journal of Distributed Sensor Networks*, 2019. 15(5): p. 1550147719850767.
26. Lhotská, L., Learning in multi-agent systems: Theoretical issues. In *International Conference on Computer Aided Systems Theory*, 1997. Springer.
27. Hernandez-Leal, P., B. Kartal, and M.E. Taylor, A survey and critique of multiagent deep reinforcement learning. *Autonomous Agents and Multi-Agent Systems*, 2019. 33(6): pp. 750–797.
28. Nguyen, T.T., N.D. Nguyen, and S. Nahavandi, Deep reinforcement learning for multiagent systems: A review of challenges, solutions, and applications. *IEEE Transactions on Cybernetics*, 2020. 50(9): pp. 3826–3839.
29. Oroojlooy, A. and D. Hajinezhad, A review of cooperative multi-agent deep reinforcement learning. *Applied Intelligence*, 2019. 53, 13677–13722.
30. Zhang, K., Z. Yang, and T. Başar, Multi-agent reinforcement learning: A selective overview of theories and algorithms. *Handbook of Reinforcement Learning and Control*, 2021: pp. 321–384.
31. Abu Talib, M. et al., Systematic literature review on Internet-of-Vehicles communication security. *International Journal of Distributed Sensor Networks*, 2018. 14(12): p. 1550147718815054.
32. Sharma, N., N. Chauhan, and N. Chand, Security challenges in Internet of Vehicles (IoV) environment. In *2018 First International Conference on Secure Cyber Computing and Communication (ICSCCC)*, 2018. IEEE.
33. Zhang, L., et al., Practical secure and privacy-preserving scheme for value-added applications in VANETs. *Computer Communications*, 2015. 71: pp. 50–60.

34. Rivas, D.A., et al., Security on VANETs: Privacy, misbehaving nodes, false information and secure data aggregation. *Journal of Network and Computer Applications*, 2011. 34(6): pp. 1942–1955.
35. Hickey, J., Vice President, Vínsula. *Telephone interview*, 2012, October.
36. Buinevich, M. and A. Vladyko, Forecasting issues of wireless communication Networks' cyber resilience for an intelligent transportation system: An overview of cyber attacks. *Information*, 2019. 10(1): p. 27.
37. Zhou, J., Zhang, S., Lu, Q., Dai, W.W., Chen, M., Liu, X., Pirttikangas, S., Shi, Y., Zhang, W., & Herrera-Viedma, E.E. A Survey on Federated Learning and its Applications for Accelerating Industrial Internet of Things. *ArXiv*, 2021. abs/2104.10501.
38. Committee, A.I.a.S., Electrical services, 2021 [cited 2022 04/04]. Available from: https://nationalindustryinsights.aisc.net.au/industries/electrotechnology/electrical-services.
39. Farsi, M., K. Ratcliff, and M. Barbosa, An overview of controller area network. *Computing & Control Engineering Journal*, 1999. 10(3): pp. 113–120.
40. Bosch, R., *CAN specification*. Robert Bosch GmbH, Postfach, 1991. p. 50.
41. Huang, J. and K.B. Kesler, *Tractor Hacking*, 2021. Available online: https://tractorhacking.github.io/ (accessed on 20/8/2023).
42. Ren, K., et al., The security of autonomous driving: Threats, defenses, and future directions. *Proceedings of the IEEE*, 2019. 108(2): pp. 357–372.
43. Bozdal, M., et al., Evaluation of can bus security challenges. *Sensors*, 2020. 20(8): p. 2364.
44. Gmiden, M., M.H. Gmiden, and H. Trabelsi, An intrusion detection method for securing in-vehicle CAN bus. In *2016 17th International Conference on Sciences and Techniques of Automatic Control and Computer Engineering (STA)*, 2016. IEEE.
45. Bozdal, M., M. Samie, and I. Jennions, A survey on can bus protocol: Attacks, challenges, and potential solutions. In *2018 International Conference on Computing, Electronics & Communications Engineering (iCCECE)*, 2018. IEEE.
46. Song, H.M., H.R. Kim, and H.K. Kim, Intrusion detection system based on the analysis of time intervals of CAN messages for in-vehicle network. In *2016 International Conference On Information Networking (ICOIN)*, 2016. IEEE.
47. Miller, C. and C. Valasek, Adventures in automotive networks and control units. *Def Con*, 2013. 21(260–264): pp. 15–31.
48. Marchetti, M. and D. Stabili, Anomaly detection of CAN bus messages through analysis of ID sequences. In *2017 IEEE Intelligent Vehicles Symposium (IV)*, 2017. IEEE.
49. Taylor, A., N. Japkowicz, and S. Leblanc, Frequency-based anomaly detection for the automotive CAN bus. In *2015 World Congress on Industrial Control Systems Security (WCICSS)*, 2015. IEEE.
50. Chandwani, A., S. Dey, and A. Mallik, Cybersecurity of onboard charging systems for electric vehicles—review, challenges and countermeasures. *IEEE Access*, 2020. 8: pp. 226982–226998.
51. Cho, K.-T. and K.G. Shin, Viden: Attacker identification on in-vehicle networks. In *Proceedings of the 2017 ACM SIGSAC Conference on Computer and Communications Security*, 2017.
52. Lu, Z., et al., LEAP: A lightweight encryption and authentication protocol for in-vehicle communications. In *2019 IEEE Intelligent Transportation Systems Conference (ITSC)*, 2019. IEEE.

53. Farag, W.A., CANTrack: Enhancing automotive CAN bus security using intuitive encryption algorithms. In *2017 7th International Conference on Modeling, Simulation, and Applied Optimization (ICMSAO)*, 2017. IEEE.
54. Jukl, M. and J. Čupera, Using of tiny encryption algorithm in CAN-Bus communication. *Research in Agricultural Engineering*, 2016. 62(2): pp. 50–55.
55. Shepherd, S.J., The tiny encryption algorithm. *Cryptologia*, 2007. 31(3): pp. 233–245.
56. Studnia, I., et al., A language-based intrusion detection approach for automotive embedded networks. *International Journal of Embedded Systems*, 2018. 10(1).
57. Jin, S., J.-G. Chung, and Y. Xu, Signature-based intrusion detection system (IDS) for in-vehicle can bus network. In *2021 IEEE International Symposium on Circuits and Systems (ISCAS)*, 2021. IEEE.
58. Larson, U.E., D.K. Nilsson, and E. Jonsson, An approach to specification-based attack detection for in-vehicle networks. In *2008 IEEE Intelligent Vehicles Symposium*, 2008. IEEE.
59. Olufowobi, H., et al., Saiducant: Specification-based automotive intrusion detection using controller area network (can) timing. *IEEE Transactions on Vehicular Technology*, 2019. 69(2): pp. 1484–1494.
60. Hoppe, T., S. Kiltz, and J. Dittmann, Applying intrusion detection to automotive it-early insights and remaining challenges. *Journal of Information Assurance and Security (JIAS)*, 2009. 4(6): pp. 226–235.
61. Ling, C. and D. Feng, An algorithm for detection of malicious messages on CAN buses. In *2012 National Conference on Information Technology and Computer Science*, 2012. Atlantis Press.
62. Weber, M., et al., Embedded hybrid anomaly detection for automotive CAN communication. In *9th European Congress on Embedded Real Time Software and Systems (ERTS 2018)*, 2018.
63. Grimm, D., M. Weber, and E. Sax, An extended hybrid anomaly detection system for automotive electronic control units communicating via ethernet. In *Proceedings of the 4th International Conference on Vehicle Technology and Intelligent Transport Systems*, 2018.
64. Kang, M.-J. and J.-W. Kang, Intrusion detection system using deep neural network for in-vehicle network security. *PLoS One*, 2016. 11(6): p. e0155781.
65. Ali, E.S., Hasan, M.K., Hassan, R., Saeed, R.A., Hassan, M.B., Islam, S., Nafi, N.S., & Bevinakoppa, S. Machine Learning Technologies for Secure Vehicular Communication in Internet of Vehicles: Recent Advances and Applications. *Security and Communication Networks*, 2021, 8868355:1-8868355:23.
66. Aboelwafa, M.M., et al., A machine-learning-based technique for false data injection attacks detection in industrial IoT. *IEEE Internet of Things Journal*, 2020. 7(9): pp. 8462–8471.
67. Khan, I.A., et al., HML-IDS: A hybrid-multilevel anomaly prediction approach for intrusion detection in SCADA systems. *IEEE Access*, 2019. 7: pp. 89507–89521.
68. Zolanvari, M., et al., Machine learning-based network vulnerability analysis of industrial Internet of Things. *IEEE Internet of Things Journal*, 2019. 6(4): pp. 6822–6834.
69. Yan, W., L.K. Mestha, and M. Abbaszadeh, Attack detection for securing cyber physical systems. *IEEE Internet of Things Journal*, 2019. 6(5): pp. 8471–8481.

70. Thomas, T., A.P. Vijayaraghavan, and S. Emmanuel, *Machine learning approaches in cyber security analytics*, 2020. Springer.
71. Talpur, A. and M. Gurusamy, Machine learning for security in vehicular networks: A comprehensive survey. *IEEE Communications Surveys & Tutorials*, 2021. 24(1): pp. 346–379.
72. Alshammari, A., et al., Classification approach for intrusion detection in vehicle systems. *Wireless Engineering and Technology*, 2018. 9(4): pp. 79–94.
73. Nazakat, I. and K. Khurshid, Intrusion detection system for in-vehicular communication. In *2019 15th International Conference on Emerging Technologies (ICET)*. 2019. IEEE.
74. Chowdhury, A., Chakravarty, T., Ghose, A., Banerjee, T., & Balamuralidhar, P. Investigations on Driver Unique Identification from Smartphone's GPS Data Alone. *Journal of Advanced Transportation*, 2018. pp. 1–11.
75. Moreira-Matias, L. and H. Farah, On developing a driver identification methodology using in-vehicle data recorders. *IEEE Transactions on Intelligent Transportation Systems*, 2017. 18(9): pp. 2387–2396.
76. Avatefipour, O., et al., An intelligent secured framework for cyberattack detection in electric vehicles' CAN bus using machine learning. *IEEE Access*, 2019. 7: pp. 127580–127592.
77. Al-Saud, M., et al., An intelligent data-driven model to secure intravehicle communications based on machine learning. *IEEE Transactions on Industrial Electronics*, 2019. 67(6): pp. 5112–5119.
78. Xiao, J., H. Wu, and X. Li, Internet of Things meets vehicles: Sheltering in-vehicle network through lightweight machine learning. *Symmetry*, 2019. 11(11): p. 1388.
79. Martínez, M.V., et al., Driving behavior signals and machine learning: A personalized driver assistance system. In *2015 IEEE 18th International Conference on Intelligent Transportation Systems*, 2015. IEEE.
80. Kieu, T., B. Yang, and C.S. Jensen, Outlier detection for multidimensional time series using deep neural networks. In *2018 19th IEEE International Conference on Mobile Data Management (MDM)*, 2018. IEEE.
81. Mao, Q., F. Hu, and Q. Hao, Deep learning for intelligent wireless networks: A comprehensive survey. *IEEE Communications Surveys & Tutorials*, 2018. 20(4): pp. 2595–2621.
82. LeCun, Y., Y. Bengio, and G. Hinton, Deep learning. *Nature*, 2015. 521(7553): pp. 436–444.
83. McMahan, B., et al., Communication-efficient learning of deep networks from decentralized data. In *Artificial Intelligence and Statistics*, 2017. PMLR.
84. Li, B., et al., DeepFed: Federated deep learning for intrusion detection in industrial cyber–physical systems. *IEEE Transactions on Industrial Informatics*, 2020. 17(8): pp. 5615–5624.
85. Zhu, K., et al., Mobile edge assisted literal multi-dimensional anomaly detection of in- vehicle network using LSTM. *IEEE Transactions on Vehicular Technology*, 2019. 68(5): pp. 4275–4284.
86. Hossain, M.D., et al., LSTM-based intrusion detection system for in-vehicle can bus communications. *IEEE Access*, 2020. 8: pp. 185489–185502.
87. Song, H.M., J. Woo, and H.K. Kim, In-vehicle network intrusion detection using deep convolutional neural network. *Vehicular Communications*, 2020. 21: p. 100198.

88. Lokman, S.F., et al., Deep contractive autoencoder-based anomaly detection for in- vehicle controller area network (CAN). In *Progress in engineering technology*, 2019. Springer. pp. 195–205.
89. Seo, E., H.M. Song, and H.K. Kim, GIDS: GAN based intrusion detection system for in-vehicle network. In *2018 16th Annual Conference on Privacy, Security and Trust (PST)*, 2018. IEEE.
90. Zhang, J., et al., Intrusion detection system using deep learning for in-vehicle security. *Ad Hoc Networks*, 2019. 95: p. 101974.
91. Lin, Y., et al., *An evolutionary deep learning anomaly detection framework for in-vehicle networks-CAN bus.* IEEE Transactions on Industry Applications, 2020. 1: pp. 1–14.
92. Yang, Y., Z. Duan, and M. Tehranipoor, Identify a spoofing attack on an in-vehicle CAN bus based on the deep features of an ECU fingerprint signal. *Smart Cities*, 2020. 3(1): pp. 17–30.
93. Cortes, C. and V. Vapnik, Support-vector networks. *Machine Learning*, 1995. 20(3): pp. 273–297.
94. Zhang, X., et al., Soil liquefaction prediction based on bayesian optimization and support vector machines. *Sustainability*, 2022. 14(19): p. 11944.
95. Patle, A. and D.S. Chouhan, SVM kernel functions for classification. In *2013 International Conference on Advances in Technology and Engineering (ICATE)*, 2013. IEEE.
96. Safavian, S.R. and D. Landgrebe, A survey of decision tree classifier methodology. *IEEE Transactions on Systems, Man, and Cybernetics*, 1991. 21(3): pp. 660–674.
97. Song, Y.-Y. and L. Ying, Decision tree methods: Applications for classification and prediction. *Shanghai Archives of Psychiatry*, 2015. 27(2): p. 130.
98. Faris, H., Hassonah, M., Al-Zoubi, A., Mirjalili, S., & Aljarah, I. A multi-verse optimizer approach for feature selection and optimizing SVM parameters based on a robust system architecture. *Neural Computing and Applications*, 2018. 30: pp. 2355–2369. https://doi.org/10.1007/s00521-016-2818-2.
99. Hearst, M. A., Dumais, S. T., Osuna, E., Platt, J., & Scholkopf, B. Support vector machines. *IEEE Intelligent Systems and their applications*, 1998. 13(4): pp. 18–28.
100. Hsu, C. W., Chang, C. C., & Lin, C. J. *A practical guide to support vector classification*, 2003.
101. Hofmann, T., Schölkopf, B., & Smola, A. J. *Kernel methods in machine learning*, 2008.
102. Breiman, L., Random Forests. *Machine Learning*, 2001. 45(1): pp. 5–32.
103. Peterson, L.E., K-nearest neighbor. *Scholarpedia*, 2009. 4(2): p. 1883.
104. Akanbi, O.A., I.S. Amiri, and E. Fazeldehkordi, *Chapter 3—research methodology.* In O.A. Akanbi, I.S. Amiri, and E. Fazeldehkordi, (Eds.), *A machine-learning approach to phishing detection and defense*, 2015. Syngress: Boston. pp. 35–43.
105. Lewis, D.D., Naive (Bayes) at forty: The independence assumption in information retrieval. In *Machine learning: ECML-98*, 1998. Springer Berlin Heidelberg: Berlin, Heidelberg.
106. Itchhaporia, D., et al., Artificial neural networks: Current status in cardiovascular medicine. *Journal of the American College of Cardiology*, 1996. 28(2): pp. 515–521.

107. Alom, M.Z., et al., A state-of-the-art survey on deep learning theory and architectures. *Electronics*, 2019. 8(3): p. 292.
108. Phung, V.H. and E.J. Rhee, A deep learning approach for classification of cloud image patches on small datasets. *Journal of Information and Communication Convergence Engineering*, 2018. 16(3): pp. 173–178.
109. Xin, Y., et al., Machine learning and deep learning methods for cybersecurity. *IEEE Access*, 2018. 6: pp. 35365–35381.
110. Gers, F.A., J. Schmidhuber, and F. Cummins, Learning to Forget: Continual Prediction with LSTM. *Neural Computation*, 2000. 12(10): pp. 2451–2471.
111. Graves, A., et al., A novel connectionist system for unconstrained handwriting recognition. *IEEE Transactions on Pattern Analysis and Machine Intelligence*, 2009. 31(5): pp. 855–868.
112. Graves, A. and J. Schmidhuber, Framewise phoneme classification with bidirectional LSTM networks. In *Proceedings. 2005 IEEE International Joint Conference on Neural Networks*, 2005.
113. Wu, X., et al., Top 10 algorithms in data mining. *Knowledge and Information Systems*, 2008. 14(1): pp. 1–37.
114. Matarić, M. J., *The robotics primer.* Intelligent Robotics and Autonomous Agents series, 2007. MIT Press, Cambridge, USA.
115. Haidegger, T., Taxonomy and standards in robotics. In *Encyclopedia of robotics*, 2021. Springer Nature: Berlin, Germany. pp. 1–10.
116. Murphy, R.R., *Introduction to AI robotics*, 2019, MIT Press.
117. Bartoš, M., V. Bulej, M. Bohušík, J. Stanček, V. Ivanov, and P. Macek, An overview of robot applications in automotive industry. *Transportation Research Procedia*, 2021. 55: pp. 837–844.

Appendix

https://github.com/Ahmed-Alruwaili/AVs-Security/blob/master/Lightwight_IDS_.ipynb

Importing Libraries

```
import pandas as pd
import matplotlib.pyplot as plt
import seaborn as sns
import warnings warnings.filterwarnings('ignore')
from sklearn.preprocessing import MinMaxScaler
from sklearn.naive_bayes import GaussianNB
from sklearn.preprocessing import LabelEncoder
from sklearn.model_selection import train_test_split
from sklearn.svm import SVC
from sklearn.tree import DecisionTreeClassifier
from sklearn.ensemble import RandomForestClassifier
from sklearn.metrics import accuracy_score, classification_report,
  confusion_matrix
from sklearn.neighbors import KNeighborsClassifier
from tensorflow.keras.layers import LSTM, Dense,
  SimpleRNN, Convolution1D
from sklearn.preprocessing import MinMaxScaler
from tensorflow.keras.models import Sequential
import numpy as np
import csv
threshold = t = 1
```

Loading the Dataset

```
from google.colab import drive
drive.mount("/content/drive")

df1 = pd.read_csv('/content/drive/MyDrive/datasets/DoS_
   dataset.csv',
   names = ['CAN ID', 'DLC', 'DATA[0]', 'DATA[1]',
            'DATA[2]', 'DATA[3]', 'DATA[4]', 'DATA[5]',
            'DATA[6]', 'DATA[7]', 'Flag'])
```

```
df2 = pd.read_csv('/content/drive/MyDrive/datasets/Fuzzy_
  dataset.csv',
  names = ['CAN ID', 'DLC', 'DATA[0]', 'DATA[1]',
          'DATA[2]', 'DATA[3]', 'DATA[4]', 'DATA[5]',
          'DATA[6]', 'DATA[7]', 'Flag'])
df3 = pd.read_csv('/content/drive/MyDrive/datasets/gear_
  dataset.csv',
  names = ['CAN ID', 'DLC', 'DATA[0]', 'DATA[1]',
          'DATA[2]', 'DATA[3]', 'DATA[4]', 'DATA[5]',
          'DATA[6]', 'DATA[7]', 'Flag'])
df4 = pd.read_csv('/content/drive/MyDrive/datasets/RPM_
  dataset.csv',
  names = ['CAN ID', 'DLC', 'DATA[0]', 'DATA[1]',
          'DATA[2]', 'DATA[3]', 'DATA[4]', 'DATA[5]',
          'DATA[6]', 'DATA[7]', 'Flag'])
```

```
Mounted at /content/drive
```

```
list_ = []
csv.register_dialect('skip_space', skipinitialspace=True)
with open('/content/drive/MyDrive/datasets/normal_run_
  data.txt', 'r') as f: reader=csv.reader(f , delimiter=' ',
  dialect='skip_space')
  for item in reader:
    list_.append(item)

normal_run_data = pd.DataFrame(list_)
normal_run_data.drop([0,1,2,4,5], axis = 1, inplace = True)
normal_run_data.columns = ['CAN ID','DLC','DATA[0]',
  'DATA[1]', 'DATA[2]', 'DATA[3]', 'DATA[4]', 'DATA[5]',
  'DATA[6]', 'DATA[7]']
normal_run_data['Flag'] = 'R'

# merging all the 5 datasets
df = pd.concat([df1,df2,df3,df4, normal_run_data])
```

Exploratory Data Analysis

```
print('DoS dataset shape : ', df1.shape)
print('Fuzzy dataset shape : ', df2.shape)
print('Gear dataset shape : ', df3.shape)
print('RPM dataset shape : ', df4.shape)
print('Normal run data shape : ', normal_run_data.shape)
```

```
  DoS dataset shape : (3665771, 11)
  Fuzzy dataset shape : (3838860, 11)
  Gear dataset shape : (4443142, 11)
  RPM dataset shape : (4621702, 11)
  Normal run data shape : (988872, 11)

# Shape of the dataset df.shape
# Distribution of the target variable that is Flag
target = df['Flag'].value_counts().sort_index()
fig_width = 1000 / 300 # ≈ 3.333 inches
fig_height = fig_width
plt.figure(figsize=(fig_width, fig_height), dpi=300)
sns.barplot(
  x=target.index,
  y=target.value,
  edgecolor='black,
  linewidth=1.5,
  palette=palette)
plt.title('Target Distribution',fontsize=20)
plt.xlabel('Flag', fontsize=15)
plt.ylabel('Count, fontsize=15)
plt.xticks(fontsize=12)
plt.yticks(fontsize=12)
plt.tight_layout()
plt.show()
```

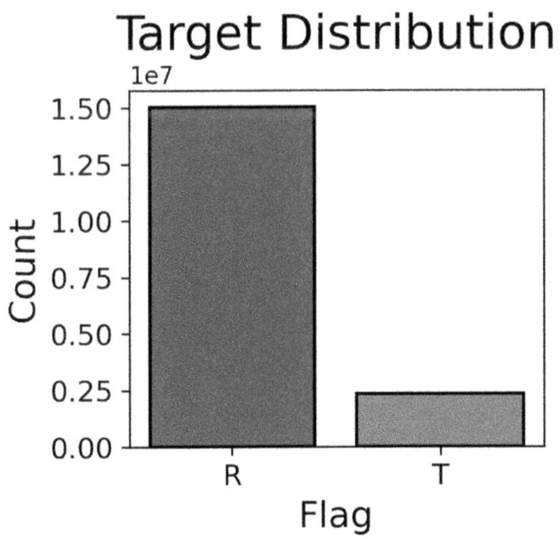

```
# Data types of all the columns of the dataset
df.info()

<class 'pandas.core.frame.DataFrame'>
Float64Index: 17558347 entries, 1478198376.389427 to
988871.0 Data columns (total 11 columns):
```

#	*COLUMN*	*DTYPE*
0	CAN ID	object
1	DLC	object
2	DATA[0]	object
3	DATA[1]	object
4	DATA[2]	object
5	DATA[3]	object
6	DATA[4]	object
7	DATA[5]	object
8	DATA[6]	Object
9	DATA[7]	Object
10	Flag	object

```
dtypes: object(11)
memory usage: 1.6+ GB

# summary statistics for all the columns
df.describe(include = 'object')
```

	CAN ID	*DLC*	*DATA [0]*	*DATA [1]*	*DATA [2]*	*DATA [3]*	*DATA [4]*	*DATA [5]*	*DATA [6]*	*DATA [7]*	*FLAG*
count	17558346	17558346	17558346	17558346	17548217	17401006	17401006	17350400	17296949	17296946	17357682
unique	2048	7	256	256	257	256	256	257	257	256	2
top	0316	8	00	00	00	00	00	00	00	00	R
freq	1481995	16368810	5793523	6936263	9526345	7441374	7235336	5981003	9899470	8936383	15026165

Dataset Preparation

1. Data Cleaning

```
# Check for the missing
values df.isnull().sum()
```

CAN ID	1
DLC	1
DATA[0]	1
DATA[1]	1
DATA[2]	10130
DATA[3]	157341
DATA[4]	157341
DATA[5]	207947
DATA[6]	261398
DATA[7]	261401
Flag	200665

```
dtype: int64

df[df.duplicated()].shape

# Check for incorrect values in the dataset column
DATA[2] as R is not the valid value for this bit column
df[df['DATA[2]']=='R']

    (16573115, 11)
```

	CAN ID	*DLC*	*DATA[0]*	*DATA[1]*	*DATA[2]*	*DATA[3]*	*DATA[4]*	*DATA[5]*	*DATA[6]*	*DATA[7]*	*FLAG*
1.478198e+09	05f0	2	01	00	R	NaN	NaN	NaN	NaN	NaN	NaN
1.478198e+09	05f0	2	01	00	R	NaN	NaN	NaN	NaN	NaN	NaN
1.478198e+09	05f0	2	01	00	R	NaN	NaN	NaN	NaN	NaN	NaN
1.478198e+09	05f0	2	01	00	R	NaN	NaN	NaN	NaN	NaN	NaN
1.478198e+09	05f0	2	01	00	R	NaN	NaN	NaN	NaN	NaN	NaN
...	...	...	...	...	...	...	...	...	...	...	...
1.478201e+09	05f0	2	01	00	R	NaN	NaN	NaN	NaN	NaN	NaN
1.478201e+09	05f0	2	01	00	R	NaN	NaN	NaN	NaN	NaN	NaN
1.478201e+09	05f0	2	01	00	R	NaN	NaN	NaN	NaN	NaN	NaN
1.478201e+09	05f0	2	01	00	R	NaN	NaN	NaN	NaN	NaN	NaN
1.478201e+09	05f0	2	01	00	R	NaN	NaN	NaN	NaN	NaN	NaN

```
# removing those incorrect data
df = df[df['DATA[2]']!='R']
df = df[df['DATA[6]']!='R']
df = df[df['DATA[5]']!='R']
df.dropna(inplace = True)
# Removing DLC column as it has only one value 8 in it
try:
  df.drop('DLC', axis = 1, inplace = True)
  except:
    pass
# Removing duplicates if any
df.drop_duplicates(inplace = True)

# Making the dataset balanced to remove biasing and overfitting
 of the models
df_T = df[df['Flag'] == 'R']
df_R = df[df['Flag'] == 'T'].iloc[:df_T.shape[0],]

df = pd.concat([df_R,df_T])

t=654 # adjust the threshold
# Converting the hexadecimal values to
decimal values for col in df.columns[:-1]:
  df[col] = df[col].apply(lambda x: int(str(x),16))

#df['Flag'].value_counts()
df['CAN ID'].describe()
```

count	908764.000000
mean	805.947920
std	522.835131
min	0.000000
25%	305.000000
50%	654.000000
75%	1118.000000
max	2047.000000

```
Name: CAN ID, dtype: float64

fig,ax =plt.subplots(2,4,figsize=(20,8))

ax[0,0].hist(df['DATA[0]'],color='blue',
edgecolor ='k') ax[0,0].set_title('CAN ID')
```

```
ax[0,1].hist(df['DATA[1]'],color='orange', edgecolor ='k')
ax[0,1].set_title('DATA[1]')

ax[0,2].hist(df['DATA[2]'],color='green', edgecolor ='k')
ax[0,2].set_title('DATA[2]')

ax[0,3].hist(df['DATA[3]'],color='purple', edgecolor ='k')
ax[0,3].set_title('DATA[3]')

ax[1,0].hist(df['DATA[4]'],color='blue', edgecolor ='k')
ax[1,0].set_title('DATA[4]')

ax[1,1].hist(df['DATA[5]'],color='orange', edgecolor ='k')
ax[1,1].set_title('DATA[5]')

ax[1,2].hist(df['DATA[6]'],color='green', edgecolor ='k')
ax[1,2].set_title('DATA[6]')

ax[1,3].hist(df['DATA[7]'],color='purple', edgecolor ='k')
ax[1,3].set_title('DATA[7]')

fig.subplots_adjust(top=0.9)
fig.suptitle('Distribution of Different Data Bits',fontsize=20)

plt.show()
```

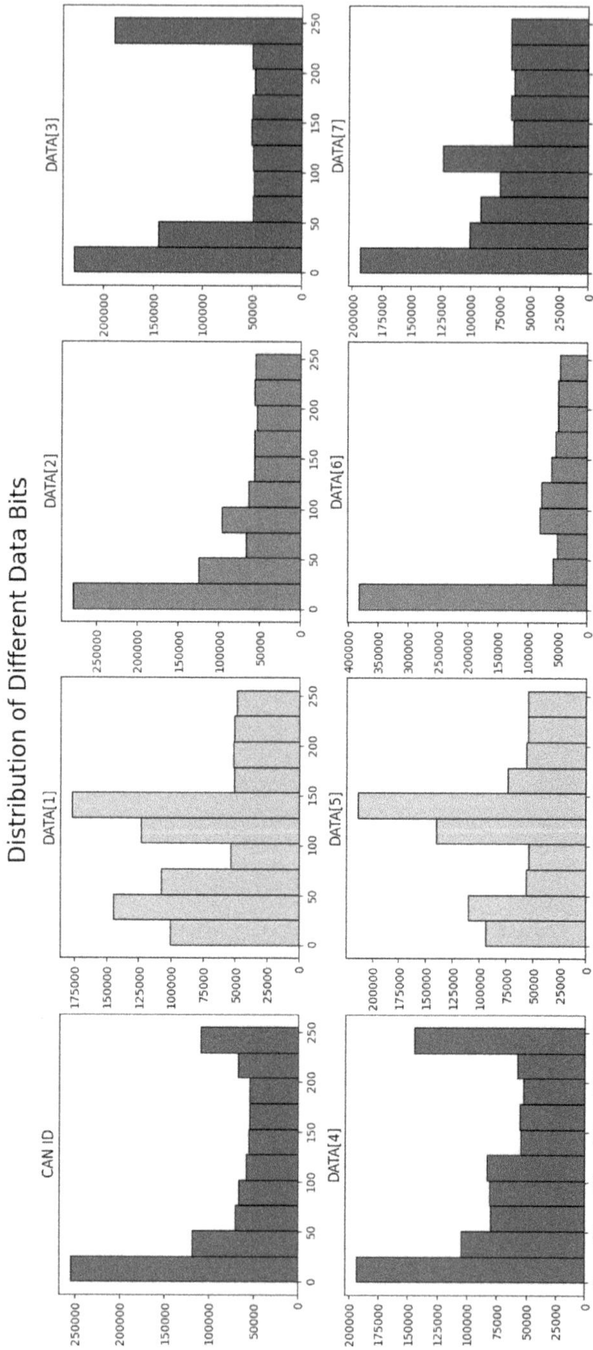
Distribution of Different Data Bits
CAN ID
DATA[1]
DATA[2]
DATA[3]
DATA[4]
DATA[5]
DATA[6]
DATA[7]

```
f,ax=plt.subplots(figsize=(10,8))
plt.title('Correlation between the different features',
  fontsize = 20)
sns.heatmap(df.corr(),annot=True,linecolor="blue",
  fmt=".2f",ax=ax)
plt.show()
```

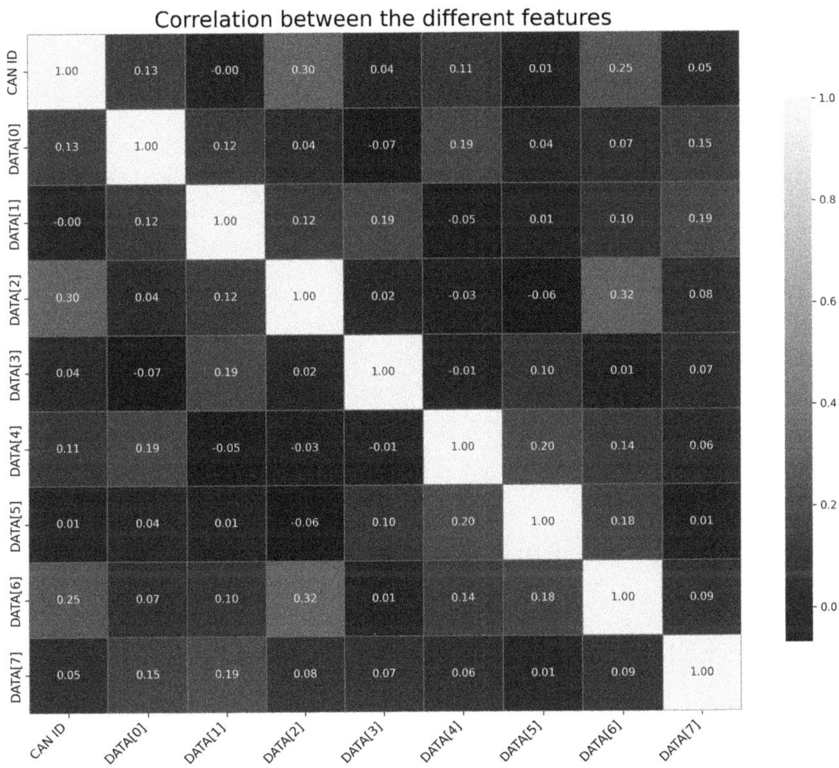

2. Data Transformation

```
# Label encoding the target variable and converting
R, T into 0,1 en = LabelEncoder()
df['Flag'] = en.fit_transform(df['Flag'])
# The threshold has been set at 1 theoretically to demonstrate
the priority of messages
ML_dataset = df[df['CAN ID']>=t]
DL_dataset = df[df['CAN ID']<t]

# Splitting into X(features) and y(target)
X_ml = ML_dataset.drop('Flag', axis = 1)
y_ml = ML_dataset[['Flag']]

# Splitting the dataset into train, test data
X_train, X_test, y_train, y_test = train_test_split(X_ml,
  y_ml, test_size=0.2, random_state = 42)

# Normalizing the
dataset scaler =
MinMaxScaler()
X_train_scaled = scaler.fit_transform(X_train)
X_test_scaled = scaler.transform(X_test)

ML_dataset.shape
  (454475, 10)

X_train.shape
  (363580, 9)

X_test.shape
  (90895, 9)
```

Machine Learning Modelling

1. Support Vector Machine

```
# Initializing the model
svm = SVC(C = 1.5, kernel = 'rbf',random_state = 42)

# Fitting on the train dataset
svm.fit(X_train_scaled, y_train)

# Making predictions on the test data
predictions = svm.predict(X_test_scaled)
```

```
# Model Evaluation
accuracy_svm = round(accuracy_score(y_test, predictions)*100,3)
print('Accuracy Score of SVM : ', accuracy_svm)
print('-'*50)
print('Classification Report : ')
print(classification_report(y_test, predictions))
print('-'*50)
cm = confusion_matrix(y_test, predictions)

sensitivity = cm[0,0]/(cm[0,0]+cm[0,1])
print('Sensitivity : ', sensitivity)

specificity = cm[1,1]/(cm[1,0]+cm[1,1])
print('Specificity : ', specificity)
```

```
Accuracy Score of SVM 99.919
```

Classification Report:

	precision	recall	f1-score	support
0	1.00	1.00	1.00	29227
1	1.00	1.00	1.00	61668
accuracy			1.00	90895
macro avg	1.00	1.00	1.00	90895
weighted avg	1.00	1.00	1.00	90895

```
Sensitivity : 0.9997604954323057
Specificity : 0.9989135370046053
```

2. *Random Forest Classifier*

```
# Initializing the model
rfc = RandomForestClassifier(criterion = 'gini',
  n_estimators =10, max_depth = 3, random_state = 42)

# Fitting on the train dataset
rfc.fit(X_train_scaled, y_train)

# Making predictions on the test data
predictions = rfc.predict(X_test_scaled)

# Model Evaluation
accuracy_rfc = round(accuracy_score(y_test, predictions)*100,3)
print('Accuracy Score of Random Forest Classifier : ',
accuracy_rfc)
print('-'*50)
```

```
print('Classification Report : ')
print(classification_report(y_test, predictions))
print('-'*50)
cm = confusion_matrix(y_test, predictions)

sensitivity = cm[0,0]/(cm[0,0]+cm[0,1])
print('Sensitivity : ', sensitivity)

specificity = cm[1,1]/(cm[1,0]+cm[1,1])
print('Specificity : ', specificity)
```

```
Accuracy Score of Random Forest Classifier : 97.423
```

Classification Report:

	precision	recall	f1-score	support
0	0.94	0.98	0.96	29227
1	0.99	0.97	0.98	61668
accuracy			0.97	90895
macro avg	0.97	0.97	0.97	90895
weighted avg	0.97	0.97	0.97	90895

```
Sensitivity : 0.9770075615013515
Specificity : 0.9729195044431471
```

3. KNN Classifier

```
# Initializing the model
knn = KNeighborsClassifier(n_neighbors = 5, weights =
'distance')

# Fitting on the train dataset
knn.fit(X_train_scaled, y_train)

# Making predictions on the test data

predictions = knn.predict(X_test_scaled)

# Model Evaluation
accuracy_knn = round(accuracy_score(y_test, predictions)*100,3)
print('Accuracy Score of K Neighbors Classifier : ', accuracy_knn)
print('-'*50)
print('Classification Report : ')
print(classification_report(y_test, predictions))
print('-'*50)
cm = confusion_matrix(y_test, predictions)
```

```
sensitivity = cm[0,0]/(cm[0,0]+cm[0,1])
print('Sensitivity : ', sensitivity)

specificity = cm[1,1]/(cm[1,0]+cm[1,1])
print('Specificity : ', specificity)
```

```
Accuracy Score of K Neighbors Classifier : 99.828
```

Classification Report:

	precision	recall	f1-score	support
0	0.99	1.00	1.00	29227
1	1.00	1.00	1.00	61668
accuracy			1.00	90895
macro avg	1.00	1.00	1.00	90895
weighted avg	1.00	1.00	1.00	90895

```
Sensitivity : 0.9997262804940638
Specificity : 0.99760005189077
```

4. Decision Tree Classifier

```
# Initializing the model
dct = DecisionTreeClassifier(max_depth = 3, random_state = 42)

# Fitting on the train dataset
dct.fit(X_train_scaled, y_train)

# Making predictions on the test data
predictions = dct.predict(X_test_scaled)

# Model Evaluation
accuracy_dct = round(accuracy_score(y_test, predictions)*100,3)
print('Accuracy Score of Decision Tree Classifier : ', accuracy_dct)
print('-'*50)
print('Classification Report : ') print(classification_
report(y_test, predictions))
print('-'*50)
cm = confusion_matrix(y_test, predictions)

sensitivity = cm[0,0]/(cm[0,0]+cm[0,1])
print('Sensitivity : ', sensitivity)

specificity = cm[1,1]/(cm[1,0]+cm[1,1])
print('Specificity : ', specificity)
```

```
Accuracy Score of Decision Tree Classifier : 97.065
```

```
Classification Report:
              precision    recall  f1-score   support

           0       0.93      0.99      0.96     29227
           1       0.99      0.96      0.98     61668

    accuracy                           0.97     90895
   macro avg       0.96      0.97      0.97     90895
weighted avg       0.97      0.97      0.97     90895
```

```
Sensitivity : 0.9853902213706505
Specificity : 0.9636602451838879
```

5. *Naïve Bayes Classifier*

```
# Initializing the model

gnb = GaussianNB()

# Fitting on the train dataset
gnb.fit(X_train_scaled, y_train)

# Making predictions on the test data
predictions = gnb.predict(X_test_scaled)

# Model Evaluation
accuracy_gnb = round(accuracy_score(y_test, predictions)*100,3)
print('Accuracy Score of Naïve Bayes Classifier : ', accuracy_gnb)

print('-'*50)
print('Classification Report : ')
print(classification_report(y_test, predictions))
print('-'*50)
cm = confusion_matrix(y_test, predictions)

sensitivity = cm[0,0]/(cm[0,0]+cm[0,1])
print('Sensitivity : ', sensitivity)

specificity = cm[1,1]/(cm[1,0]+cm[1,1])
print('Specificity : ', specificity)
```

```
Accuracy Score of Naive Bayes Classifier : 96.11
```

Classification Report:

	precision	recall	f1-score	support
0	0.92	0.97	0.94	29227
1	0.98	0.96	0.97	61668
accuracy			0.96	90895
macro avg	0.95	0.96	0.96	90895
weighted avg	0.96	0.96	0.96	90895

```
Sensitivity : 0.9659903513874157
Specificity : 0.9587792696374132

accuracy_scores = [accuracy_svm, accuracy_rfc, accuracy_knn,
accuracy_dct, accuracy_gnb]
model_names = ['Support \nVector Machine','Random Forest
\nClassifier',
  'K Nearest \nNeighbors' ,'Decision Tree \nClassifier',
  'Naive Bayes \nClassifier']

plt.figure(figsize=(15,5))
plt.grid(b=True, which='major', axis='y')
plt.title('Comparing Accuracy of ML Models',fontsize=15)
colors=['red','orange','green','magenta','blue']
plt.xticks(fontsize=12)
plt.yticks(fontsize=12)
plt.ylabel('Accuracy',fontsize=12)
plt.xlabel('Models',fontsize=12)
bar = plt.bar(model_names,accuracy_scores,edgecolor='black',
color=colors, linewidth=2, alpha =0.5)
def autolabel(rects):
  for rect in rects:
    h = rect.get_height()
    plt.text(rect.get_x()+rect.get_width()/2,
    0.5*(h), '%f'%(h),
      ha='center', va='bottom',fontsize=15)
autolabel(bar)
```

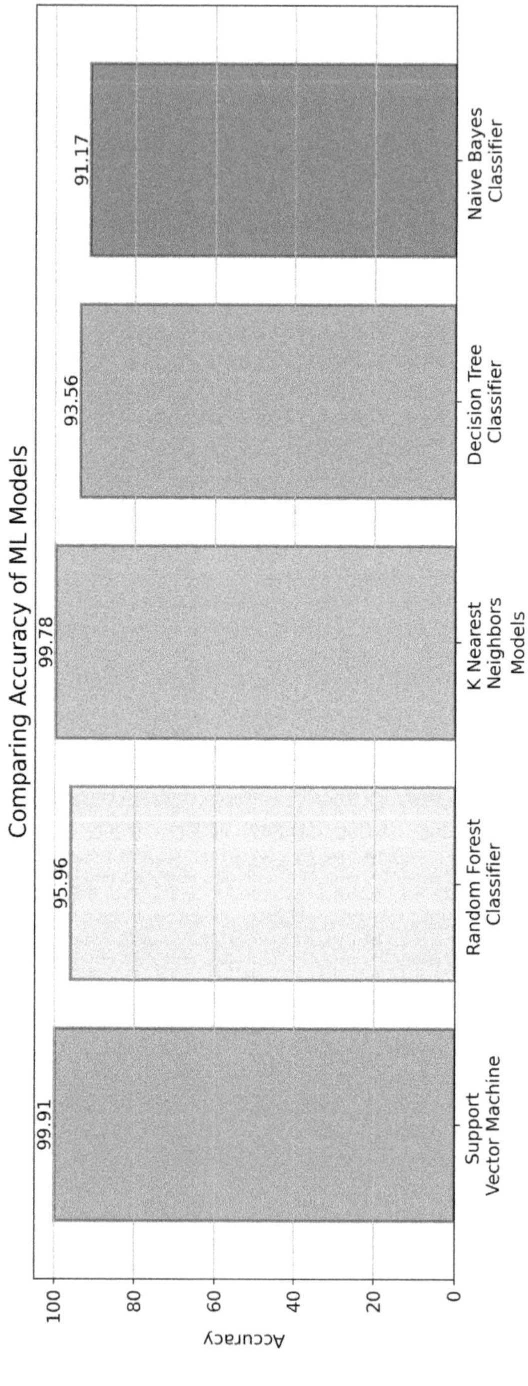
Comparing Accuracy of ML Models
Accuracy
0
20
40
60
80
100
99.91
95.96
99.78
93.56
91.17
Support Vector Machine
Random Forest Classifier
K Nearest Neighbors Models
Decision Tree Classifier
Naive Bayes Classifier

Deep Learning Modelling

```
# Splitting into X(features) and y(target)
X_dl = DL_dataset.drop('Flag', axis = 1)
y_dl = DL_dataset[['Flag']]

# Splitting the dataset into train, test data
X_train, X_test, y_train, y_test = train_test_split(X_dl,
y_dl, test_size=0.2, random_state = 42)

# Normalizing the dataset
scaler = MinMaxScaler()
X_train_scaled = scaler.fit_transform(X_train)
X_test_scaled = scaler.transform(X_test)

# Reshaping for fitting into the deep learning models
x_train = np.reshape(X_train_scaled, (X_train_scaled.
shape[0],X_train_scaled.shape[1],1))
x_test = np.reshape(X_test_scaled, (X_test_scaled.
shape[0],X_test_scaled.shape[1],1))


DL_dataset.shape

X_train.shape
  (454289, 10)
  (363431, 9)

X_test.shape
  (90858, 9)
```

1. Simple Neural Network

```
# Initializing model
nn = Sequential()

# Input layer with 256 units
nn.add(Dense(256, input_dim=x_train.shape[1], activation =
'tanh'))
nn.add(Dense(128, activation = 'tanh'))
nn.add(Dense(64, activation = 'tanh'))
nn.add(Dense(1, activation ='sigmoid'))
```

```
# defining loss function, optimizer, metrics and then
compiling model nn.compile(loss='binary_crossentropy',
optimizer='adam',metrics=['accuracy'])

# training the model on training dataset
history = nn.fit(x_train, y_train, epochs=10, batch_
size=64,validation_data=(x_test, y_test))

Epoch 1/10
5679/5679 [==============================] - 31s 5ms/step -
loss: 0.0320 - accuracy: 0.9889 - val_loss: 0.0073 - val_
accuracy: 0.9980 Epoch 2/10
5679/5679 [==============================] - 28s 5ms/step -
loss: 0.0054 - accuracy: 0.9986 - val_loss: 0.0047 - val_
accuracy: 0.9989 Epoch 3/10
5679/5679 [==============================] - 25s 4ms/step -
loss: 0.0037 - accuracy: 0.9990 - val_loss: 0.0029 - val_
accuracy: 0.9993
Epoch 4/10
5679/5679 [==============================] - 29s 5ms/step -
loss: 0.0026 - accuracy: 0.9993 - val_loss: 0.0031 - val_
accuracy: 0.9992 Epoch 5/10
5679/5679 [==============================] - 27s 5ms/step -
loss: 0.0022 - accuracy: 0.9993 - val_loss: 0.0027 - val_
accuracy: 0.9993 Epoch 6/10
5679/5679 [==============================] - 27s 5ms/step -
loss: 0.0018 - accuracy: 0.9995 - val_loss: 0.0014 - val_
accuracy: 0.9997 Epoch 7/10
5679/5679 [==============================] - 31s 6ms/step -
loss: 0.0018 - accuracy: 0.9995 - val_loss: 0.0016 - val_
accuracy: 0.9996
Epoch 8/10
5679/5679 [==============================] - 26s 4ms/step -
loss: 0.0014 - accuracy: 0.9996 - val_loss: 0.0024 - val_
accuracy: 0.9994 Epoch 9/10
5679/5679 [==============================] - 28s 5ms/step -
loss: 0.0014 - accuracy: 0.9996 - val_loss: 0.0016 - val_
accuracy: 0.9996 Epoch 10/10
5679/5679 [==============================] - 28s 5ms/step -
loss: 0.0012 - accuracy: 0.9997 - val_loss: 0.0011 - val_
accuracy: 0.9997
```

```
# Evaluation

predictions = nn.predict(x_test)
prediction = []
for i in predictions:
  if i[0]>0.5:
    prediction.append(1)
  else:
    prediction.append(0)
accuracy_nn = round(accuracy_score(y_test, prediction)*100,3)
print('Test Accuracy of Neural Network : ', accuracy_nn)
print('-'*50)
print('Classification Report : ')
print(classification_report(y_test, prediction)) print('-'*50)
cm = confusion_matrix(y_test, prediction)

sensitivity = cm[0,0]/(cm[0,0]+cm[0,1])
print('Sensitivity : ', sensitivity)

specificity = cm[1,1]/(cm[1,0]+cm[1,1])
print('Specificity : ', specificity)

2840/2840 [==============================] - 5s 2ms/step

Test Accuracy of Neural Network 99.969
```

Classification Report:

	precision	recall	f1-score	support
0	1.00	1.00	1.00	61828
1	1.00	1.00	1.00	29030
accuracy			1.00	90858
macro avg	1.00	1.00	1.00	90858
weighted avg	1.00	1.00	1.00	90858

```
Sensitivity : 0.9999514782946238
Specificity : 0.9991388219083707
```

2. Long Short-Term Memory

```
# Initializing model

lst = Sequential()

# input layer and LSTM layer with 256 neurons
lst.add(LSTM(units=256, return_sequences=True, input_shape=
(x_train.shape[1],1))) lst.add(Dense(128, activation = 'tanh'))
lst.add(Dense(64, activation = 'tanh'))
lst.add(Dense(32, activation = 'tanh'))
# output layer with sigmoid activation
lst.add(Dense(1, activation='sigmoid'))

# defining loss function, optimizer, metrics and then
compiling model lst.compile(loss='binary_crossentropy',
optimizer='adam',metrics=['accuracy'])

# training the model on training dataset
history = lst.fit(x_train, y_train, epochs=10, batch_
size=64,validation_data=(x_test, y_test))

Epoch 1/10
5679/5679 [==============================] - 353s 62ms/
step - loss: 0.1909 - accuracy: 0.9186 - val_loss: 0.0991 -
val_accuracy: 0.9675 Epoch 2/10
5679/5679 [==============================] - 339s 60ms/
step - loss: 0.0620 - accuracy: 0.9791 - val_loss: 0.0422 -
val_accuracy: 0.9868
Epoch 3/10
5679/5679 [==============================] - 354s 62ms/
step - loss: 0.0432 - accuracy: 0.9867 - val_loss: 0.0309 -
val_accuracy: 0.9913 Epoch 4/10
5679/5679 [==============================] - 352s 62ms/
step - loss: 0.0409 - accuracy: 0.9882 - val_loss: 0.0758 -
val_accuracy: 0.9783 Epoch 5/10
5679/5679 [==============================] - 353s 62ms/
step - loss: 0.0346 - accuracy: 0.9902 - val_loss: 0.0234 -
val_accuracy: 0.9924 Epoch 6/10
5679/5679 [==============================] - 355s 62ms/
step - loss: 0.0300 - accuracy: 0.9915 - val_loss: 0.0392 -
val_accuracy: 0.9889
Epoch 7/10
5679/5679 [==============================] - 355s 63ms/
step - loss: 0.0275 - accuracy: 0.9921 - val_loss: 0.0203 -
val_accuracy: 0.9935 Epoch 8/10
```

```
5679/5679 [===============================] - 358s 63ms/
step - loss: 0.0277 - accuracy: 0.9923 - val_loss: 0.0180 -
val_accuracy: 0.9944 Epoch 9/10
5679/5679 [===============================] - 362s 64ms/
step - loss: 0.0272 - accuracy: 0.9924 - val_loss: 0.0232 -
val_accuracy: 0.9930
Epoch 10/10
5679/5679 [===============================] - 353s 62ms/
step - loss: 0.0296 - accuracy: 0.9915 - val_loss: 0.0216 -
val_accuracy: 0.9931

# Evaluation
predictions = lst.predict(x_test)
prediction = []
for i in predictions:
  if i[0]>0.5:
    prediction.append(1)
  else:
    prediction.append(0)

accuracy_lst = round(accuracy_score(y_test, prediction)*100,3)

print('Test Accuracy of LSTM : ', accuracy_lst)
print('-'*50)
print('Classification Report : ')
print(classification_report(y_test, prediction))
print('-'*50)
cm = confusion_matrix(y_test, prediction)

sensitivity = cm[0,0]/(cm[0,0]+cm[0,1])
\ print('Sensitivity : ', sensitivity)

specificity = cm[1,1]/(cm[1,0]+cm[1,1])
print('Specificity : ', specificity)

2840/2840 [=============================] - 43s 15ms/step
```

Test Accuracy of LSTM *96.539*

Classification Report:

	precision	recall	f1-score	support
0	0.96	0.99	0.97	61828
1	0.97	0.92	0.94	29030
accuracy			0.97	90858
macro avg	0.97	0.95	0.96	90858
weighted avg	0.97	0.97	0.97	90858

```
Sensitivity : 0.9866565310215436
Specificity : 0.9200826730967964
```

3. Recurrent Neural Network

```
# Initializing model
rnn = Sequential()

# input layer and RNN layer with 128 neurons
rnn.add(SimpleRNN(units=256, return_sequences=True, input_
shape=(x_train.shape[1],1)))

rnn.add(Dense(128, activation = 'relu'))
rnn.add(Dense(64, activation = 'relu'))
rnn.add(Dense(32, activation = 'relu'))
# output layer with sigmoid activation
rnn.add(Dense(1, activation='sigmoid'))

# defining loss function, optimizer, metrics and then
compiling model rnn.compile(loss='binary_crossentropy',op
timizer='adam',metrics=['accuracy']) #rnn.compile(loss=0.1,
optimizer='adam',metrics=['accuracy'])

# training the model on training dataset
history = rnn.fit(x_train, y_train, epochs=10, batch_
size=64,validation_data=(x_test, y_test))

Epoch 1/10
5679/5679 [==============================] - 149s 26ms/
step - loss: 0.1188 - accuracy: 0.9540 - val_loss: 0.0619 -
val_accuracy: 0.9792
Epoch 2/10
5679/5679 [==============================] - 139s 24ms/
step - loss: 0.0647 - accuracy: 0.9765 - val_loss: 0.0626 -
val_accuracy: 0.9789
Epoch 3/10
5679/5679 [==============================] - 140s 25ms/
step - loss: 0.0475 - accuracy: 0.9850 - val_loss: 0.0377 -
val_accuracy: 0.9884
Epoch 4/10
5679/5679 [==============================] - 134s 24ms/
step - loss: 0.0397 - accuracy: 0.9886 - val_loss: 0.0412 -
val_accuracy: 0.9878
Epoch 5/10
5679/5679 [==============================] - 141s 25ms/
step - loss: 0.0341 - accuracy: 0.9903 - val_loss: 0.0322 -
val_accuracy: 0.9907
Epoch 6/10
```

```
5679/5679 [==============================] - 140s 25ms/
step - loss: 0.0331 - accuracy: 0.9907 - val_loss: 0.0228 -
val_accuracy: 0.9929
Epoch 7/10
5679/5679 [==============================] - 134s 24ms/
step - loss: 0.0312 - accuracy: 0.9913 - val_loss: 0.0269 -
val_accuracy: 0.9930
Epoch 8/10
5679/5679 [==============================] - 146s 26ms/
step - loss: 0.0303 - accuracy: 0.9915 - val_loss: 0.0213 -
val_accuracy: 0.9940
Epoch 9/10
5679/5679 [==============================] - 137s 24ms/
step - loss: 0.0288 - accuracy: 0.9920 - val_loss: 0.0198 -
val_accuracy: 0.9942
Epoch 10/10
5679/5679 [==============================] - 135s 24ms/
step - loss: 0.0281 - accuracy: 0.9921 - val_loss: 0.0197 -
val_accuracy: 0.9942

# Evaluation

predictions = rnn.predict(x_test)
prediction = []
for i in predictions:
  if i[0]>0.5:
    prediction.append(1)
  else:
    prediction.append(0)
accuracy_rnn = round(accuracy_score(y_test, prediction)*100,3)
print('Test Accuracy of RNN : ', accuracy_rnn)
print('-'*50) print('Classification Report : ')
print(classification_report(y_test, prediction))
print('-'*50)
cm = confusion_matrix(y_test, prediction)

sensitivity = cm[0,0]/(cm[0,0]+cm[0,1])
print('Sensitivity : ', sensitivity)

specificity = cm[1,1]/(cm[1,0]+cm[1,1])
print('Specificity : ', specificity)

2840/2840 [==============================] - 23s 8ms/step
```

```
Test Accuracy of RNN : 97.311
```

Classification Report:

	precision	recall	f1-score	support
0	0.97	0.99	0.98	61828
1	0.97	0.94	0.96	29030
accuracy			0.97	90858
macro avg	0.97	0.97	0.97	90858
weighted avg	0.97	0.97	0.97	90858

```
Sensitivity : 0.9866565310215436
Specificity : 0.9442645539097485
```

4. *Convolution Neural Network*

```
# Initializing model
cnn = Sequential()

# Input layer with CNN with 128 neurons
cnn.add(Convolution1D(256, kernel_size=3, activation='tanh',
input_shape=(x_train.shape[1],1)))

# Hidden layers with 100 and 64 units and tanh as activation
function
cnn.add(Dense(128, activation='tanh'))
cnn.add(Dense(64, activation='tanh'))
cnn.add(Dense(32, activation='tanh'))

# output layer with sigmoid activation
cnn.add(Dense(1, activation='sigmoid'))

# defining loss function, optimizer, metrics and then
compiling model cnn.compile(loss='binary_crossentropy',op
timizer='adam',metrics=['accuracy'])

# training the model on training dataset
history = cnn.fit(x_train, y_train, epochs=10, batch_
size=64,validation_data=(x_test, y_test),)

Epoch 1/10
5679/5679 [==============================] - 60s 9ms/step -
loss: 0.2493 - accuracy: 0.8975 - val_loss: 0.1720 - val_
accuracy: 0.9328 Epoch 2/10
```

```
5679/5679 [================================] - 58s 10ms/
step - loss: 0.1625 - accuracy: 0.9369 - val_loss: 0.1580 -
val_accuracy: 0.9378 Epoch 3/10
5679/5679 [================================] - 56s 10ms/
step - loss: 0.1483 - accuracy: 0.9426 - val_loss: 0.1435 -
val_accuracy: 0.9453 Epoch 4/10
5679/5679 [================================] - 51s 9ms/step -
loss: 0.1398 - accuracy: 0.9458 - val_loss: 0.1337 - val_
accuracy: 0.9479
Epoch 5/10
5679/5679 [================================] - 57s 10ms/
step - loss: 0.1337 - accuracy: 0.9478 - val_loss: 0.1365 -
val_accuracy: 0.9481 Epoch 6/10
5679/5679 [================================] - 58s 10ms/
step - loss: 0.1279 - accuracy: 0.9502 - val_loss: 0.1276 -
val_accuracy: 0.9507 Epoch 7/10
5679/5679 [================================] - 53s 9ms/step -
loss: 0.1234 - accuracy: 0.9522 - val_loss: 0.1207 - val_
accuracy: 0.9534
Epoch 8/10
5679/5679 [================================] - 57s 10ms/
step - loss: 0.1197 - accuracy: 0.9540 - val_loss: 0.1147 -
val_accuracy: 0.9558 Epoch 9/10
5679/5679 [================================] - 51s 9ms/step -
loss: 0.1169 - accuracy: 0.9554 - val_loss: 0.1240 - val_
accuracy: 0.9534 Epoch 10/10
5679/5679 [================================] - 54s 9ms/step -
loss: 0.1144 - accuracy: 0.9565 - val_loss: 0.1114 - val_
accuracy: 0.9576

# Evaluation

predictions = cnn.predict(x_test)
prediction = []
for i in predictions:
  if i[0]>0.5:
    prediction.append(1)
  else:
    prediction.append(0)
accuracy_cnn = round(accuracy_score(y_test, predic-
tion)*100,3)
print('Test Accuracy of CNN : ', accuracy_cnn)
print('-'*50)
```

```
print('Classification Report : ')
print(classification_report(y_test, prediction))
print('-'*50)
cm = confusion_matrix(y_test, prediction)

sensitivity = cm[0,0]/(cm[0,0]+cm[0,1])
print('Sensitivity : ', sensitivity)

specificity = cm[1,1]/(cm[1,0]+cm[1,1])
print('Specificity : ', specificity)

2840/2840 [==============================] - 10s 3ms/step

Test Accuracy of CNN : 97.582
```

Classification Report:

	precision	recall	f1-score	support
0	0.97	1.00	0.98	61828
1	0.99	0.93	0.96	29030
accuracy			0.98	90858
macro avg	0.98	0.96	0.97	90858
weighted avg	0.98	0.98	0.98	90858

```
Sensitivity : 0.996441741605745
Specificity : 0.9318980365139511

accuracy_scores = [accuracy_nn, accuracy_lst, accuracy_rnn,
accuracy_cnn]
model_names = ['Neural Network', 'Long Short Term\nMemory',
              'Recurrent Neural \nNetwork', 'Convolution
              Neural \nNetwork']

plt.figure(figsize=(10,5))
plt.grid(b=True, which='major', axis='y')
plt.title('Comparing Accuracy of DL Models',fontsize=15)
colors=['red','orange','green','magenta']
plt.xticks(fontsize=12)
plt.yticks(fontsize=12)
plt.ylabel('Accuracy',fontsize=12)
plt.xlabel('Models',fontsize=12)
```

```
bar = plt.bar(model_names,accuracy_scores,edgecolor='black',
color=colors, linewidth=2, alpha =0.5) def autolabel(rects):
  for rect in rects:
    h = rect.get_height()
    plt.text(rect.get_x()+rect.get_width()/2, 0.5*(h), '%f'%(h),
      ha='center', va='bottom',fontsize=15)
autolabel(bar)
```

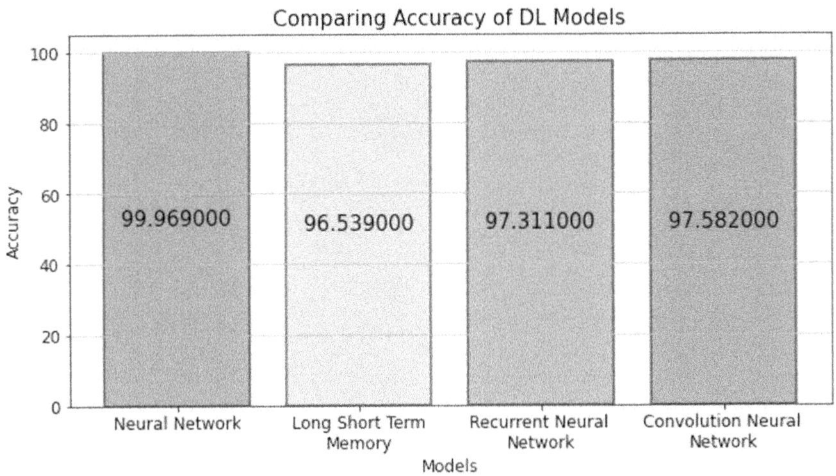

Index

For Product Safety Concerns and Information please contact our EU representative GPSR@taylorandfrancis.com
Taylor & Francis Verlag GmbH, Kaufingerstraße 24, 80331 München, Germany

www.ingramcontent.com/pod-product-compliance
Ingram Content Group UK Ltd.
Pitfield, Milton Keynes, MK11 3LW, UK
UKHW022109190926
475702UK00013B/1333
* 9 7 8 1 0 0 3 6 1 0 9 1 5 *